Leadership Development Program Manual

3rd Edition

Jane C. Chauvin, Ph.D.

Gifted EDUCATION

Leadership Development Program Manual, 3rd Edition

Editing: Molly A. Isaacs-McLeod, JD, LL.M.
Cover Design: Kelly Crimi
Interior Design: The Printed Page

Published by
Gifted Unlimited, LLC
12340 U.S. Highway 42, No. 453
Goshen, KY 40026
www.giftedunlimitedllc.com

ISBN 978-1-953360-14-4

Printed and bound in the United States of America.

Contents

Tribute to Frances Karnes

I met Dr. Frances Karnes at the University of Southern Mississippi where I received my Ph.D. Frances was my academic advisor and the director of my dissertation. She was the one who urged me to focus my dissertation on leadership since, of the five areas of giftedness acknowledged by the United States Office of Education, it was the one that had the least written about it in publications devoted to Gifted Education.

Almost immediately after I had finished my graduate work, Frances suggested that I start work on a program to develop leadership characteristics in middle and high school age children and youth. She offered to collaborate with me on this work. We primarily used the research that I had studied and written about in my dissertation as the basis for the Leadership Development Instrument and the accompanying manual of activities. Of course, as we wrote, we incorporated any other research on leadership that we could find.

Without Frances' encouragement and willingness to work with me on this, the LSI and its manual might never have been published. Frances was far better known than I was in the field of gifted studies and her name lent credibility to the work that we did together.

Unfortunately, she was not able to be a partner in this 3rd Edition of the Leadership Development Program and the Leadership Development Instrument. As I wrote and updated and revised things, she was always with me in spirit. She was my advisor, my mentor, and my friend.

Jane C. Chauvin, Ph.D.
New Orleans, Louisiana
April 2022

Section I: Introduction

All cultures need leaders, and it is important to identify and develop leadership skills and abilities in children and youth, as well as in adults. Occupational fields of medicine, technology, education, religion, business and industry, politics, and the arts all need people who can possess intelligence, creativity, and critical thinking skills, and know how to use them. Parents and educators have critical roles in assisting in the development of leadership attitudes and skills.

It is important to identify, measure, and cultivate key components of leadership potential, and it is for such purposes that the present work has been written. Karnes and Bean (1990) specifically described these components, and subsequent work by Karnes and Chauvin (2000b) has led to the creation of this Leadership Development Program and its associated *Leadership Skills Inventory*—a method by which students can self-assess their leadership skills in several key areas and compare their skills in these areas. As of 2020, the *Leadership Skills Inventory* has been used in all 50 states, as well as eight countries outside the United States. The present version is the third (3rd) update of this program.

Characteristics of Leadership in Youth with High Leadership Potential

Leadership is a skill that comes largely from what Howard Gardner (1983) has labeled interpersonal intelligence—knowledge of oneself and others. In fact, leadership has been designated a talent area in federal and state definitions of gifted students since the Marland Report was issued by the U.S. Department of Education in 1971.

Schools and other agencies wishing to nurture and develop leadership must provide specific activities and differentiated programs for students. Yet despite its importance in our culture, leadership behaviors for students remains the least discussed and included of the curricular areas in the literature, and even the concept and dimensions of leadership are not well defined.

Few school programs seek to identify those students who have high leadership potential, nor do schools incorporate leadership education into their curricula. Yet many students truly have high potential in leadership skills such that they can be called "gifted" in this area. Though all students can profit from leadership training, the characteristics of such gifted youth enable them particularly to profit from leadership development. Students with unusually high leadership potential show many or all of the following characteristics or skills:

- Flexibility and efficiency in thought and action.
- Perception of others' perspectives.

- ❍ Ability to motivate and influence others.
- ❍ Tolerance of ambiguities.
- ❍ A thirst for knowledge and desire for challenge.
- ❍ Self-directedness.
- ❍ Self-assurance.
- ❍ Verbal and expressive skills.
- ❍ Ability to tolerate ambiguity
- ❍ Ability to show compassion and empathy for others.
- ❍ Creativity and problem-solving skills.
- ❍ Critical analytical reasoning skills.

Parents and the Development of Leadership

Preparing young people for leadership responsibility begins in the home with an enriched environment that offers opportunities for children to acquire broad interests, increase self-esteem, and develop the insights and skills that characterize leaders. Parents and guardians can provide their children with support and encouragement as they participate in a wide variety of home and community activities. In these activities, children can be encouraged to plan and carry out daily choices. For example, parents and guardians should encourage their children to be involved in the selection, planning, execution, and evaluation of family activities ranging from a day at the zoo to a vacation overseas. Youngsters should also be encouraged to plan, initiate, and complete a variety of self-evaluated individual projects. These future skills of leadership are not learned automatically. They must be patiently taught and modeled by parents in the home.

Discussion and debate about current events and other topics foster independent thinking and nurture leadership potential, and they are frequent occurrences in families whose children later become eminent (Goertzel, Goertzel, Goertzel, & Hansen, 2004). Parents who listen openly and thoughtfully without expecting children to embrace their social, political, and economic views are demonstrating leadership characteristics. Mutual respect, objectivity, empathy, and understanding are highly valued by gifted young people, particularly those who need a safe place to test their ideas.

Opportunities for decision making at an early age will help to foster the critical reasoning skills necessary to be an effective leader. Inappropriate decisions by children and youth, although difficult for parents to accept, allow them to experience the consequences of their decisions, and such experiences often enhance their ability to evaluate themselves more accurately about their future decision-making skills.

Schools and the Development of Leadership

Leadership concepts and skills and leadership development can be infused into the curriculum in all academic areas, including the fine and performing arts. For example, thematic curriculum units and reading lists should include biographies and autobiographies of outstanding leaders. Students can be encouraged to analyze and evaluate the motivation, contributions, and influences of each leader, as well as assessing the leadership styles employed. Major events, as well as family and other influences that were important in the life of each leader, can be highlighted. Here are some examples of ways to incorporate leadership aspects into various curricula areas.

Sciences

Physical and biological sciences, mathematics, and social sciences provide unique opportunities for projects in which initiating, planning, critical thinking, creative problem solving, and decision making can be developed. They are rich with opportunities to learn about leaders who have influenced such areas as government and politics, science and technology, humanities and the arts, business and industry, philosophy and religion, and health science and medicine. Students can learn how their own interests, passions, and abilities can develop into careers. They can study how the contributions of others relate to values, including to their own value systems. For example, many leaders in scientific fields have been concerned about poverty and the human condition.

Humanities

Language Arts, Speech, Literature, History, and other courses that emphasize oral and written communication provide opportunities for potential leaders to learn how to present ideas succinctly, clearly, and persuasively. Preparing and presenting speeches or oral reports, listening to, and critiquing presentations, writing news reports and editorials for school and other local publications, preparing for and engaging in debates, leading conference and discussion sessions, and participating in school and other election campaigns are only a few of the many options available. Group activities provide opportunities for young people to learn how to listen to others, help others feel important and valued, accept their contributions, keep discussions relevant, and practice working collaboratively as well as leading.

Arts

Students can learn leadership skills and gain inspiration from talented people of the past and present who have enriched all of us through their contributions in the fine and performing arts. Their creative works, the trends they initiated, and the enduring results of their efforts are worthy of study, as are their lives and the circumstances under which their work came to fruition.

Other School Options for Leadership Development

Several strategies strengthen and broaden educational experiences for youth who are gifted in leadership abilities. Instructional units on leadership development can be provided at each grade level in a resource room or pullout administrative arrangement. Some secondary schools offer structured credit courses on leadership or have special seminars for members of student government. Mentorships and internship programs provide opportunities for youth to work with adult community leaders who are willing to help identify, develop, and nurture future leaders.

All of these are opportunities to have students prepare and periodically update personal plans for their own leadership development, including descriptions of how they intend to obtain the experiences set forth in their plans. The value of this experience is enhanced when students share individual plans in group sessions, brief the group on their purpose, revise plans if the critique brings forth acceptable suggestions, report to peers on progress made after following the plans for a period of time, and evaluate the plans using self-designed criteria.

Leadership through Extracurricular Activities

Since leadership is learned over time through involvement with others, extracurricular activities provide fertile ground for nurturing future leaders. Group participation offers unique opportunities for young people to belong, support others, and learn a variety of leadership styles. Students learn how to encourage others, to create a cooperative environment with group spirit, and to resolve conflict. They begin to understand diverse attitudes, skills, and talents, as well as how to interact effectively with a diversity of people while working toward a common goal.

Although there are many organized extracurricular activities for youth, those who want to develop their leadership potential can do so through fewer formal methods. Individuals or groups can plan special projects or a leadership plan by setting goals, objectives, and timelines toward a mission of improving some area of the school or community. Skills such as seeking all available information, defining a group task, and devising a workable plan may be developed through any community project. No matter how small or large the goal, the process involved in devising and implementing the plan develops leadership potential.

Leadership is much more than being elected or appointed to a position, and it is acquired most effectively through practice. Educators, parents, and other concerned adults who are interested in the development of youth who show leadership abilities can make a difference in the lives of these students by providing them with opportunities to realize their leadership potential.

Section II: The Leadership Development Program and the LSI

Admittedly, leadership is hard to define and to measure. Research in interpersonal giftedness, a dimension that includes leadership, has tended to focus on an individual's socializing with a group or the group's impact on the individual. The results of that research have demonstrated that measures of leadership are not as exact as most other types of giftedness for which standardized tests are available.

To help with this problem, and to provide a basis for a program to develop leadership skills, the *Leadership Skills Inventory* was created. The *Leadership Skills Inventory* was developed as a way for students to self-assess their abilities in various key areas of leadership; activities were then developed that were keyed to the specific items within the *Leadership Skills Inventory*. These activities are intended to help youth develop leaderships skills.

Different styles of leadership, such as laissez faire, democratic, and authoritarian, have been recognized. The *Leadership Skills Inventory* does not seek to train students in a particular style of leadership, but rather seeks to develop skills that research has shown are needed by all leaders.

The inclusion of leadership in the United States Office of Education (USOE) definition of giftedness underlines the correlation that some have felt exists between talent in social leadership and above average intelligence (Tannenbaum, 1983). This widely accepted definition thus highlights the need felt by many to encourage the ablest to come forward and use their talents for the greater good of all. In any society, the encouragement and training of those with special talents has strengthened the welfare of all. The relationship between leadership and giftedness has also been buoyed by Howard Gardner (1983), who described interpersonal intelligence as a distinct intelligence in his theory of "multiple intelligences," and by Daniel Goleman (1995), who emphasized that "emotional intelligence" is as important as academic intelligence for life success.

Purpose of the *Leadership Skills Inventory*

The *Leadership Skills Inventory* is a self-administered, self-scored inventory of personal leadership skills designed for use with individuals across a broad age range. It can be used with students at the upper elementary or secondary levels, as well as individuals at post-secondary levels who aspire to improve their potential for leadership roles. The *Leadership Skills Inventory* is designed to help individuals ascertain their abilities within nine skill areas of leadership:

- Fundamentals of leadership.

- ❍ Written communication skills.
- ❍ Speech communication skills.
- ❍ Character-building skills.
- ❍ Decision-making skills.
- ❍ Group dynamics.
- ❍ Problem-solving skills.
- ❍ Personal development.
- ❍ Planning skills.

After completing the inventory, individuals will be able to determine their strengths and weaknesses in each of the specific areas. An accompanying profile sheet allows the individual to identify graphically the areas in which additional skill development is needed.

Several important results can develop from the use of the *Leadership Skills Inventory*:

1. Individuals will have a better understanding of the skills necessary for leadership.
2. Individuals will realistically assess their current leadership skills. The self-reporting and self-scoring format allows individuals to obtain a more objective view of themselves, rather than being rated by others who may be less knowledgeable about individual strengths and weaknesses.
3. Individuals will receive immediate feedback regarding their leadership skills, rather than having to wait for two or three weeks to obtain the results. Therefore, areas that need to be developed or improved can receive immediate attention.
4. Individuals will have a record of their present leadership skills to use as a basis for comparison and as a measure of progress as they work on activities to improve their self-reported areas of weakness.
5. Persons responsible for the administration of the inventory will be able to use the results to plan a program of leadership skills development based on the areas of indicated need. The *Leadership Skills Inventory* thus serves the purpose of a needs' assessment instrument.

Scales Comprising the *Leadership Skills Inventory*

The derivation of the items and scales for the *Leadership Skills Inventory* is based on a review of the professional literature in the field of leadership. From this base of knowledge, it has been determined that skills necessary for leadership development can be classified into nine categories. The nine categories—or scales—included in the inventory and a brief explanation of each are listed below.

1. Fundamentals of Leadership (FL)—skills that include defining terms and identifying various leadership styles.
2. Written Communication Skills (WCS)—skills that include outlining, writing a speech, and doing research reports.
3. Speech Communication Skills (SCS)—skills that include defining one's viewpoint on issues, delivering a speech, and offering constructive criticism.

4. Character-Building Skills (CBS)—skills that include understanding the importance of free choice, identifying things that one values and prizes, and affirming one's choices.
5. Decision-Making Skills (DMS)—skills that include gathering facts, analyzing the consequences of certain decisions, and reaching logical conclusions.
6. Group Dynamic Skills (GDS)—skills that include serving as a group facilitator, effecting compromise, and achieving consensus.
7. Problem-Solving Skills (PSS)—skills that include identifying problems, revising strategies for problem solving, and accepting unpopular decisions.
8. Personal Skills (PERS)—skills that include self-confidence, sensitivity, and personal grooming.
9. Planning Skills (PS)—skills that include setting goals, developing timelines, and formulating evaluation strategies.

Uses of the *Leadership Skills Inventory*

The *Leadership Skills Inventory* has broad-based utility within schools, as well as other settings in the community. Within upper elementary, secondary, or post-secondary schools, the inventory will be useful to teachers, administrators, and counselors. Additionally, the *Leadership Skills Inventory* can assist persons who are guiding the growth and development of individuals in special classes or clubs that focus on the leadership development of its members. Individuals in student government organizations and other student groups will benefit from use of the *Leadership Skills Inventory*. English and social studies teachers will find many uses for the instrument.

Beyond the school setting, the following community leaders will find the *Leadership Skills Inventory* useful in assisting with the leadership potential of their members or employees:

- Directors of youth organizations.
- Leaders of religious, civic, and social organizations.
- Personnel development specialists in education, health and social services, and business and industry.
- Persons directly involved in leadership training and management.
- Individuals desiring their own self-improvement in the area of leadership.

Administering the *Leadership Skills Inventory*

The *Leadership Skills Inventory* can be administered in a wide variety of group situations, or it can be administered individually. Administration time for the entire inventory is approximately 45 minutes. Since the inventory is untimed, it may be given in one sitting, or it may be administered over several shorter periods. No special training is required to administer the inventory, but persons who administer it should be generally familiar with its contents.

The reading level of the inventory is suitable for most individuals at the upper elementary level and is such that the *Leadership Skills Inventory* can also be used with individuals who have higher reading levels. If a reading problem is perceived, however, or if the instrument is administered to individuals with special needs, the inventory may be given orally. In such situations, the administrator should be careful to match the oral reading to the working speed of the individual or group.

Required Materials

The administrator of the *Leadership Skills Inventory* will need a copy of this manual, the *Leadership Skills Inventory* individual form, and a supply of pencils and/or pens.

Specific Administration Directions

Each individual taking the inventory should be directed to complete the personal information on the first page of the individual form. After the individual completes that information, the administrator should read aloud the following directions, which are printed on the first page of the individual form:

> *This inventory is made up of statements that focus on the knowledge and skills of leadership. Please understand that this is an inventory and not a test. Its purpose is to help you learn about your abilities in leadership skills. There are no right or wrong answers. For each statement, mark the response that is true for you. Do not skip an item. Read each statement carefully, and then check ( ) the one response that best describes your skills.*

- Check ALMOST ALWAYS if you usually possess this knowledge or skill.
- Check ON MANY OCCASIONS if you frequently possess this knowledge or skill.
- Check ONCE IN A WHILE if you occasionally possess this knowledge or skill.
- Check ALMOST NEVER if you rarely possess this knowledge or skill.

Scoring the *Leadership Skills Inventory*

Individuals may score their own forms. Scoring each of the nine scales of the *Leadership Skills Inventory* is easily accomplished in five steps. The raw scores for each scale are marked directly on the *Leadership Skills Inventory* Profile Sheet. By looking at the left or right margins of the *Leadership Skills Inventory* Profile Sheet, the raw scores can be converted to standard T-scores, thus allowing the scale scores to be easily compared with each other. A sample *Leadership Skills Inventory* Profile Sheet is shown on the next page. Step-by-step directions follow.

Step 1: Enter the numerical response for each item statement in the column labeled "Item Value" on the right side of the *Leadership Skills Inventory* individual form.

Step 2: For each scale, sum the item raw scores, and write that score at the bottom of the page on the line beside "Total Points." For each of the nine scales, write the "Total Points" for that scale in the appropriate "Raw Score" blank at the bottom of the *Leadership Skills Inventory* Profile Sheet, which is the last page in the *Leadership Skills Inventory*.

Step 3: Plot the raw score total for each scale on the profile sheet by placing a circle around the appropriate raw score value in the column directly above each scale's raw score. Connect the circles with an unbroken line to form a graph.

Step 4: Convert the raw score of each scale to a standard T-score by looking at the T-score column on the extreme left or right margin of the profile sheet. The T-scores are standard scores that have a mean of 50 and a standard deviation of 10. These T-scores can be used, if desired, for later statistical analyses.

Step 5: Evaluate any scales that fall above or below the mean score (T=50). When scores are below the average, the students may require instructional attention in those areas. The lower the scores are below a T-score of 50, the more likely they are to be significant and to require specific skill practice.

LEADERSHIP SKILLS INVENTORY PROFILE SHEET

Leadership Development Program

Frances A. Karnes, Ph.D.
Jane C. Chauvin, Ph.D.

T SCORE	FL	WCS	SCS	CBS	DMS	GDS	PSS	PERS	PS	T SCORE
75										75
70	27 26	36 35	42 41 40 39			57 55 56	18		51 50 49	70
65										65
60	25 24 23 22	34 33 32 31 30 29 28	38 37 36 35 34 33 32 31 30	51 50 49 48 47 46 45 44	30 29 28 27 26 25	54 53 52 51 49 50 48 47 46 45 43 44	17 16 15 14	63 62 60 61 59 58 57 55 56 54 53	48 47 45 46 44 43 42 41 40 39 38	60
55										55
50	21 20 19 18	27 26 25 24 23 22 21 20	29 28 27 26 25 24 23 22	43 42 41 40 39 38 37 36 35 34	24 23 22 21 20 19 18	42 41 40 39 37 38 36 35 34 33 32	13 12 11 10	52 50 51 49 48 47 45 46 44 43 42 40 41	37 36 35 34 33 32 31 30 29 28	50
45										45
40	17 16 15 14	19 18 17 16 15 14 13 12	21 20 19 18 17 16 15 14 13	33 32 31 30 29 28 27 26 25 24	17 16 15 14 13 12	30 31 29 28 27 26 24 25 23 22 21 20	9 8 7 6	39 38 37 35 36 34 33 32 30 31 29 28	26 27 25 24 23 22 21 20 19 18 17	40
35										35
30	13 12 11 10	11 10 9 8 7 6 5	[illegible] 11 10 9 8 7 [illegible]	[illegible] 20 [illegible] 18 17 [illegible] 15 [illegible]	11 10 9 8 7 6	[illegible] 16 13 14 12 11 10 [illegible]	5 4 3 2	[illegible] 24 [illegible] 22 20 21 [illegible] 18 [illegible]	[illegible] 14 13 12 11 10 9 [illegible]	30
25										25
20	[illegible] 8 7 6 5	[illegible] 2 1 0	[illegible] 2 1 0	12 11 10 9 8 7 6 5 4 3 2 1 0	5 4 3 2 1 0	6 7 5 4 3 2 0 1	1 0	14 13 12 10 11 9 8 7 6 4 5 3 2 1 0	3 2 1 0	20
15										15
10	4 3 2 1									10
5	0									5
RAW SCORE										
T-SCORE										

Gender____ Age____ Grade____ School____

Please indicate if this is a pre-assessment ☐ or post-assessment ☐

T-Score Transformations

The standard T-Scores used in the *Leadership Skills Inventory* Profile Sheet were derived by analyzing the raw scores of the total deviation sample (see Table 1, Appendix A, p. x). The data did not suggest a need to develop separate norms for men and women. The original sample, the development, and the validation of the *Leadership Skills Inventory* are described later in this manual.

The raw score values for each *Leadership Skills Inventory* scale were converted to T-scores using the following formula and rounding the obtained value to the nearest integer value:

$$T = 50 + \frac{10\,(X-M)}{SD}$$

The raw score value is represented by X, while M and SD represent the normative group mean and standard deviation, respectively. The value of the mean for the standard scores is 50, and the standard deviation is 10. Use of T-scores in this manner allows the scales within the *Leadership Skills Inventory* to be compared directly with each other.

Interpreting the *Leadership Skills Inventory*

The *Leadership Skills Inventory* was designed to indicate areas of an individual's leadership potential that need additional development, as well as those leadership areas that are already more developed. If an individual has points on the profile that are below the scale mean, this would indicate that additional skill development is needed in those specific categories. If an individual's points on the profile fall above the scale mean, this would suggest an above average level of skill development in that area of leadership.

It appears, due to the high mean scores obtained across the normative sample, that the inventory is better able to discriminate individual differences at the lower end of each scale. Thus, although high points on certain scales might indicate already-developed abilities that an individual may wish to use, the *Leadership Skills Inventory* appears more sensitive to identifying areas that could use improvement.

Although the *Leadership Skills Inventory* items are organized into separate scales, it is recognized that each scale likely has sub-components within it. Thus, when developing instructional programs, an individual item analysis in each category is suggested in order to pinpoint areas of strength or weakness more specifically. To assist in this, specific instructional activities are provided for each item of each scale on the inventory in Section III of this *Leadership Development Program* manual.

Development of the *Leadership Skills Inventory*

A thorough review of the literature pertaining to leadership revealed that the skills necessary to be a leader fall into nine categories. For each area, self-assessment items were generated and written by the authors. To establish content validity, two panels for review were used. Adults working to develop leadership in youth constituted one group of reviewers. Professional persons working with student council, scouting (boys and girls), gifted education, and elementary and secondary education were represented.

The second review group was composed of youth representing the above organizations. After both reviews were completed, suggestions were incorporated. Some items were deleted; other items were revised.

The *Leadership Skills Inventory* was originally published in 1985 by D.O.K. and later by Pro-Ed. During the intervening years, the *Leadership Skills Inventory* was widely used by students and teachers across the country. In 2000, Karnes and Chauvin published a revision of the *Leadership Skills Inventory* based upon the data that had been collected through repeated use of the instrument in various programs, but particularly those in the summer Leadership Studies Program which has been conducted for youth at The University of Southern Mississippi for the past 15 years. Attention was paid to updating terms and re-writing items to include more current research findings and social trends. The republishing of this instrument and the accompanying updated version of the manual are a reply to the public's interest in and use of this publication. The third update (2021) of the *Leadership Skills Inventory* concentrates on vocabulary, diversity, and the inclusion of technology.

Samples Used in Developing the Leadership Skills Inventory

Eight samples of students were obtained in seven states, giving broad geographic representation for the development of the *Leadership Skills Inventory*. These states were California, Illinois, Kansas, Louisiana, Massachusetts, Mississippi, and Nebraska. Teachers were contacted, and directions were given for the administration of the inventory. All of the teachers contacted agreed to participate in the field-testing, and they were sent the needed number of inventories and the preliminary manual that described the purpose of the instrument and guidelines for administration. After administering the inventories, the teachers returned the marked copies.

The total sample was composed of 452 students, of which 422 reported their gender. Of that group, 207 were males and 215 were females. The ages of the total sample ranged from nine to 18 years old, with a mean of 14.6 years (see Table 1, Appendix A, p. x). The contribution to the total sample by the various states is as follows.

A sample of 56 (20 males and 36 females) from California was taken from English classes in a public school. The ages of these students ranged from 16 to 17 years, with a mean age of 16.4 (see Table 2, Appendix A, p. x).

Fifty-nine subjects who were enrolled in a public school constituted a sample from Illinois. Nine males and 20 females reported their gender, while 30 students did not. They ranged in age from 14 to 18 and were members of English classes (see Table 3, Appendix A, p. x).

The 17 males and 10 females in a Kansas sample were enrolled in a program for gifted youth. Their ages ranged from 12 to 16, with a mean of 13.89 years (see Table 4, Appendix A, p. x).

Two samples were obtained from Louisiana. The first sample was from English classes in a private secondary school. The 45 subjects (23 males and 22 females) ranged in age from 12 to 17, with a mean age of 13.4 (see Table 5, Appendix A, p. x). These students were administered the inventory and four weeks later were readministered the instrument. Another sample from a private school in Louisiana was also included in this second sample. The 107 subjects (74 males and 33 females) ranged in age from nine to 18, with a mean age of 14.4 (see Table 6, Appendix A, p. x).

A Massachusetts sample consisted of 75 secondary public school students (26 males and 49 females). Their mean chronological age was 15.0, with a range of 12 to 17 (see Table 7, Appendix A, p. x).

The sample from Mississippi was composed of students enrolled in a class on leadership. The 24 subjects (10 males and 14 females) were 13 and 14 years old. Their mean age was 13.5 (see Table 8, Appendix A, p. x).

Fifty-nine students comprised a sample from Nebraska. The 28 males and 31 females ranged in age from 12 to 15. They were students in English classes in a public secondary school (see Table 9, Appendix A, p. x).

Reliability

The internal consistency reliability of the *Leadership Skills Inventory* was examined in a variety of ways. First, the overall internal consistency of each of the nine scales was determined. The internal consistency is reported using three methods: the split-half coefficient, the Spearman-Brown formula, and a Kuder-Richardson internal consistency formula. Also, the means and standard deviations for each of the nine scales were determined.

For the total developmental sample of 452 students, the split-half reliability coefficients ranged from .81 to .92, with a median coefficient of .85. The Spearman-Brown formula reliability coefficients ranged from .78 to .90, with a median coefficient of .84. The Kuder-Richardson internal consistency formula reliability coefficients ranged from .80 to .93, with a median coefficient of .85. These reliability coefficients appear more than adequate, particularly since five of the nine scales were composed of less than 15 items, thus reducing the likelihood of obtaining high coefficients.

Validity

Karnes and D'Ilio (1988b) report a study designed to assess criterion-related validity of the *Leadership Skills Inventory* in a group of students and in a group of adult community leaders. The student subjects were 113 girls and boys (grades 6-11) who had recently completed a one-week Leadership Studies Program based on the *Leadership Skills Inventory*. Adult subjects were 55 community leaders who were chosen by a panel to represent arts, business, government, professions, and civic activities. Both groups completed the inventory. Mean self-rating for the students who had completed the leadership training was higher than mean self-rating of adults. Results are consistent with the criterion-related validity of the instrument.

In a study of the concurrent validity of the *Leadership Skills Inventory*, 60 students enrolled in state-approved public school programs for the gifted at grades 6 and 7 were given the *Leadership Skills Inventory*. Four certified teachers of these students were simultaneously asked to complete an inventory on the leadership skills and abilities of each subject. The mean *Leadership Skills Inventory* T-scores of the students showed no significant differences from the mean teachers' ratings of leadership behaviors of these students (Karnes & D'Ilio, 1988a).

Edmunds (1998) examined the content, concurrent, and construct validity of the *Leadership Skills Inventory* with 90 academically gifted students in grade 12. Statistically significant positive correlations were found to exist between the students' *Leadership Skills Inventory* scores and other leadership indicators, thereby establishing concurrent validity, and the results of a critical semantic comparison indicated support for content validity. The nine scales of the *Leadership Skills Inventory* showed significant positive correlations with each other, suggesting that they all are measuring aspects of the leadership construct.

Impact of the Leadership Studies Program

Two studies (Karnes, 1999) investigated the long-term impact of the Leadership Studies Program—a one-week summer residential training program that uses the *Leadership Skills Inventory* and its related activities—on the leadership behavior and competencies of the participants who attended during the first five years. A survey/questionnaire was sent to 125 randomly selected former participants. Ninety individuals completed and returned the instrument. The former participants indicated that their participation in the program had greatly increased their knowledge and skills of leadership, their awareness of their potential for leadership, and their current roles as leaders in elected, appointed, and self-initiated positions.

Section III: Leadership Instructional Activities for the LSI

Leadership for the Future

The 21st Century is unfolding, and new challenges will undoubtedly arise. How will we find and nurture our potential leaders? Who will be the Churchill or the Roosevelt or the Michelle Obama or the Martin Luther King, Jr.? Who will encourage the emerging leadership of women of all color on the national and international scene? Will this new century produce other leaders like Hitler or Bin Laden? And if it does, who will save us from them? Where do strong and positive leaders come from?

No one can adequately predict who will arise as the leaders of tomorrow, but research does tell us some of the characteristics and attributes that any skillful leader must possess. All leaders are responsible for changing "what is" into "what ought to be." Those who aspire to be leaders must be guided by two important realities: (1) they must have a personal and believable vision that is also achievable, and (2) they must be willing to make a commitment to their own development as a leader. Good leaders prepare themselves well. Holding an office or accepting an appointed position does not make one a leader. Accumulating knowledge and devising solutions does.

According to Abramson (1996), gone are the "Four C's" of the last century—"Command, Control, Compartmentalize, and Cope." The 21st Century will require four new Cs of its leaders, "Communicate, Collaborate, Coach, and Catalyze." Leadership has been defined as "the ability to influence a group toward the achievement of goals" (Robbins, 1997). Leaders for the new millennium will guide others to devise solutions, not simply propose all of the answers. Waldman, Bathazard. & Peterson (2011) ask the question, "Can we revolutionize the way that inspirational leaders are identified and developed?"

Yet another noteworthy definition of leadership has been proposed by John Mariotti (1999): "Leadership is the ability to convince people to follow a path they have never taken to a place they have never been and, upon finding it to be successful, to do it over and over again." Thus, we see that motivation and risk-taking are also characteristics of leaders. Traditionally, the concept of leadership has included responsibility, high expectations for self and others, and fluent and concise self-expression. Other related skills include forecasting, decision-making, self-confidence, and organizational skills. This is echoed in an article by Larson and Angus (2011) in which they dwell on the need to teach youth to *think strategically.*

Because of the increasing multicultural aspects of the global environment, leaders of the future must respect and positively interact with varied ethnic and minority groups, and they will need to encourage and foster the participation of all segments of society. Brooms, Clark, & Smith (2018) and St. Jon, Rowley, & Hu (2009) all write about encouraging leadership in students of color as soon as possible and with a definite program that develops the skills that are necessary to attain the goals of active, purposeful, and ethical leadership.

In any discussion of leadership, accountability must be addressed. Effective leadership is accountable leadership—leadership that constantly seeks to know how the job might be better accomplished. After receiving such feedback, wise leadership adjusts its actions. An effective leader possesses humility and a respect for others. Without these characteristics, leaders evolve into dictators.

The most effective leaders must have a quality and a presence that attracts people to work with them (Mariotti, 1999, Waldman & Peterson, 2011). True leaders work with and for people, not over them. Leaders conquer fear because they believe in themselves and their visions. Will leaders of tomorrow be drastically different from the leaders of today? Probably not in terms of their characteristics, but they will have a whole new agenda with which to contend. How can we help them to be better prepared?

Activities Related to the Inventory Items

The activities found in this manual are designed to complement and enhance each of the items on the *Leadership Skills Inventory*. At least one activity is included for each item on each scale of the instrument. These activities are certainly not all-encompassing. Persons using this manual should feel free to supplement, expand, or change any activity based on the needs of the individuals involved in the program. Activities presented here are offered only as suggestions.

The authors have developed activities that should not require commercial materials or elaborate equipment. These activities use simple materials that should be readily available to almost anyone. However, a list of references is included at the end of this manual to allow teachers to see some of the publications available that could be used to enhance and supplement certain activities, even though these materials are not required for the success of the leadership program.

In this 3rd Edition of the Leadership Development Program, an effort was made to include suggestions for the use of technology in the Activities, if it is available. The authors want to make clear, however, that none of the activities are dependent on technology. Very simple materials can always be used and can be very effective.

As noted previously, the purpose of the *Leadership Skills Inventory* is to assess strengths and weaknesses in the various areas of leadership. Once the students have recorded areas that they feel need improving, the teacher may then select appropriate activities from the manual to help them remediate that area. It is not necessary to cover all of the activities; time may instead be concentrated in the areas that need the most improvement. Nor is it necessary to use the activities in the exact order that they are listed in this manual. However, if the order of the activities is changed, care must be taken that results of a previous activity are not required for the completion of any other subsequent ones. In addition, certain sections can be combined for more effective use. For example, the oral and written communication sections share several activities and would appear to be a natural combination.

Teachers/administrators/leaders, and other professionals are encouraged to expand the scope of the activities by including films, guest speakers, field trips, etc. whenever appropriate. The teacher/administrator/leader here is viewed as a facilitator whose job it is to encourage and lend support. Most activities are designed to be student-directed.

Originally, these activities were designed for use with upper elementary, secondary, and post-secondary students. They are suitable for participants of a wide variety of ages, however. With elementary-level students, some modifications in the activities may be warranted. The materials may have to be adapted to the experiential level of the students involved. Beyond the use of the activities in a school setting, those adults involved in youth associations, civic and social organizations, business and industry, and leadership training and management will find the activities beneficial in a variety of ways.

Teachers/leaders should be aware that the inventory or the activities might contain words with which younger students may not be familiar. Thus, teachers are urged to read over all activities carefully to identify any potential difficulties before using them in group situations.

Depending upon the ages, experiences, and cultural diversity of the participants, the teacher's role may vary somewhat. With older students, the teacher/leader serves more as a facilitator, while with younger, less experienced students, the teacher/leader may have to assume the role of an instructor.

Within the school setting, activities may be used in the regular classroom, special programs, and with extracurricular organizations. They may also be used in a variety of administrative arrangements—for example, as a semester course on leadership, for part of a day over an entire school year, or for a summer or Saturday program.

The major final responsibility for the teacher/leader is to observe the development of a written Plan for Leadership, which is the culminating activity in the leadership model. For this reason, it is suggested that even though the order of the activities may be altered, the Planning Skills section should always be placed last. To put the learned leadership skills into practice, the teacher should urge students to carry out their Plans for Leadership in their school, community, and/or religious affiliations.

Validation of Activities

The activities for each item within the *Leadership Skills Inventory* have been field-tested and validated in six different states, representing a cross-section of the country. States participating were Louisiana, Ohio, Illinois, North Carolina, California, and Mississippi. Students participating were in the upper elementary and secondary grades. In addition, further validation of the materials was undertaken within university-based summer programs for 16 years.

Karnes, Meriweather, and D'Ilio (1987) report the effectiveness of the instructional program with all pre-post gains significant at the $p<.01$. The increase in scores is attributed to the instructional program. For a sample of 270 students in grades 6 through 12 after completing the program during 1996, 1997, and 1998, the pre-post assessment scores on the *Leadership Skills Inventory* were significant at the $p<.001$ level (Karnes, 1999).

Leadership Instructional Activities

Scales Comprising the Leadership Skills Inventory

- Fundamentals of Leadership (FL)
- Written Communication Skills (WCS)
- Speech Communication Skills (SCS)
- Character-Building Skills (CBS)
- Decision-Making Skills (DMS)
- Group Dynamic Skills (GDS)
- Problem-Solving Skills (PSS)
- Personal Skills (PERS)
- Planning Skills (PS)

Frances A. Karnes, Ph.D.
Jane C. Chauvin, Ph.D.

Fundamentals of Leadership (FL)

1.1 I understand the meaning of the term "leader."

Materials: Paper and pen or computer or Google Documents; dictionary.

The students will write a definition of the term "leader." They will then compare their definitions and come up with a group definition. They will compare their definition of "leader" with one in a dictionary.

1.2 I understand the meaning of the term "leadership."

Materials: Paper and pen or computer or Google Documents; dictionary.

1.3 I can tell the difference between the meanings of the terms "leader" and "leadership."

Materials: The students' work from 1.1 and 1.2; a list of famous and diverse leaders with pictures or name cards of these individuals.

The students will divide into small groups and compare their definitions. One person from each group will report on differences found by his or her particular group. The total group will then come to a consensus. The teacher will place names and/or pictures of famous leaders of diverse nationalities or ethnic groups around the classroom. The students will discuss the personal characteristics of each famous leader individually. A list of positive characteristics common to all leaders will be developed.

The students will take the list and rate themselves on these characteristics. They will set personal goals for themselves in regard to the development of those characteristics in which they have a self-perceived weakness. The students will be instructed to keep this list of characteristics as a guide for working toward the development of these traits.

1.4 I am able to identify various styles of leadership.

Materials: None required.

The teacher will present information about the three leadership styles: laissez faire, democratic, and authoritarian (Appendix B, p. 71).

Three students will be selected and instructed privately to role play one of the leadership styles. The other students will not be told of the leadership style that is to be portrayed. The students not involved in the role playing will act as observers to determine the leadership styles enacted.

1.5 I can describe my own style of leadership.

Materials: Problem situations that students are to solve.

The students will be presented with fictitious problem situations and will be asked to describe how they would solve these problems/scenarios. An analysis of the methods used will be undertaken by the students in order to better understand the leadership style that they were portraying in the fictitious situation.

Different types of problems will be presented so that students can see that different styles of leadership are necessary in different situations (Appendix B, p. 71).

1.6 I can identify leadership styles of various leaders.

Materials: None required.

Students will generate a list of well-known leaders from many cultural and ethnic backgrounds. Certain students will be asked to come up and secretly select one leader from the list and role play that person. The other students will attempt to guess who the person being portrayed is and name his/her leadership style.

The students will construct a list of questions that they would use to interview someone in a leadership position to determine their leadership style. They will practice interviewing each other first and then will interview either a leader in the community or someone posing as a leader. The group will evaluate the answers obtained and seek to identify the various leadership styles represented.

The students will be assigned to read biographies and autobiographies and/or watch documentaries of famous leaders from many different backgrounds and analyze the leadership styles of each. A discussion will follow after the individual analysis.

1.7 I can identify various titles of leadership positions.

Materials: White Board and markers or computer or Google Documents.

The students as a group will identify various areas of society where leadership exists or is needed, i.e., medicine, government, etc. They will then divide into groups and formulate titles of individuals that would fit into each area.

1.8 I understand the requirements and responsibilities of various leadership positions.

Materials: Lists the students have developed in 1.7. Computer for research is optional.

The students will take the leadership titles and outline and enumerate the various duties of each leadership position.

1.9 I can identify the positive and negative aspects of being a leader.

Materials: Poster paper and magic markers or computers, or possibly using collaborative Google slides.

The students will brainstorm answers to the following questions:

a. Why would someone want to be a leader?

b. Why do people leave well-paying jobs to become government leaders?

c. What are the possible benefits of being in a leadership position?

d. What are some negative aspects of being a leader?

e. Based upon the above discussion, how would someone balance the positive and negative aspects of leadership?

The students or teacher/leader may wish to generate additional questions to add to this list.

Written Communication Skills (WCS)

2.1 I know how to get and use written information.

Materials: White Board and Markers or collaborative Google Document and Smartboard projector, if available.

The students will brainstorm sources from which to obtain information and appropriate uses of each (Appendix B, p. 72).

Suggested supplemental activity: A guest speaker will elaborate on technological advances in information systems.

2.2 I can write my ideas so that others can read and understand them.

Materials: Paper and pen or computer or Google Documents.

Each student will write key ideas for an essay or a short story on leadership. They will then develop these ideas into an essay or a short story pertaining to leadership.

The students will exchange their works and discuss them. The student reviewers will draw up a list of main ideas from the papers they have read. These lists will be compared to see what similarities exist.

2.3 I can compare and contrast ideas in my writing.

Materials: Paper and pen or computer or Google Documents.

Each student will choose two famous leaders and compare and contrast their styles in a short paper.

The students will then share the ideas which they have developed, and they will compare and contrast different leadership characteristics.

2.4 I can distinguish fact from opinion in writing.

Materials: Newspaper, magazines, or Internet articles.

The students will bring in articles from various sources and discuss what portions of these articles are fact or opinion.

The teacher/leader should present information about the purpose of editorials and contrast them with articles of a more general reporting nature.

The students will write an editorial on "Why Leadership Should Be Developed at an Early Age" or on a similar topic determined by the student and the teacher.

2.5 I can summarize written information in a clear manner.

Materials: Various issues of leading news magazines or newspaper articles.

The students will read and summarize the lead article in one of the magazines or newspapers available. They will then report on the key points presented by the author.

2.6 I can write an outline.

Materials: Paper and pen or computer or Google Documents.

The teacher will describe techniques of outlining.

Each student will outline a speech that he/she will write for the activity in 2.7.

2.7 I can write to persuade others to my point of view.

Materials: Paper and pen or computer or Google Documents.

Using the outline in 2.6, the students will write a speech on a topic of their choice pertaining to leadership.

2.8 I can write a business letter.

Materials: Paper and pen or computer or White Board and Markers or Google Documents

The teacher/leader will present the techniques of writing a business letter and will give an example (Appendix B, pp. 72-73). The students will then write a business letter.

2.9 I can write a social letter.

Materials: Paper and pen or computer or Google Documents; examples of social letters.

The teacher will discuss the techniques of writing a social letter and give an example to illustrate his/her points (Appendix B, p. 73). The students will write a "Thank You" letter.

2.10 I can prepare an agenda for a meeting.

Materials: Paper and pen or computer; Google Documents; an agenda for a meeting.

The teacher/leader will discuss why an agenda is needed, the techniques of drawing up an agenda, and give an example (Appendix B, p. 74).

The students will draw up an agenda for a meeting that they plan to hold.

2.11 I can write a speech.

Materials: Paper and pen or computer or Google Documents.

The students will outline and then write a persuasive speech to nominate themselves or someone else to a position of leadership.

2.12 I can evaluate my writing and the writing of others.

Materials: Speeches written in 2.11.

The students will swap the speeches they developed in 2.11 and will then offer suggestions for improvement.

Each student will look at the suggestions offered by the reviewer and decide which they can incorporate. They will rewrite their speeches in order to improve them.

Speech Communication Skills (SCS)

3.1 I can speak in a clear and concise manner.

Materials: Newspaper or magazine articles and paper and pen or computer.

The teacher will distribute newspaper and magazine articles to the students. They will summarize the articles and deliver their summaries orally.

3.2 I can tell others how I feel.

Materials: None required.

The students will divide into two's and relate to each other some event in their lives that had special meaning to them. The whole group will then discuss how much easier or harder it is to deal with feelings rather than facts.

3.3 I can participate in group discussions.

Materials: Headlines cut from newspapers or magazines or slips of paper with controversial issues printed on them.

The students will draw a topic. They will then divide into small groups and take turns leading a discussion on their topic. Afterward, the students will identify the leadership style the leaders were attempting to use. A recorder for each group should be appointed (this will be necessary for 3.4).

3.4 I can summarize the ideas of the group and express them.

Materials: The notes of the recorders for each group in 3.3.

One student will have been assigned the job of recorder in each small group. At the end of the session, the recorder will summarize the discussion which took place. Other students will critique the summaries to make sure they cover all important points.

3.5 I can tell both sides of an argument without allowing my own feelings to show.

Materials: White Board and markers; paper and pen or computers; Google Documents.

The students will make a list of controversial issues and discuss how both sides can be presented objectively. They will then discuss: How important is this skill to a leader? When might such occasions arise?

3.6 I can state and defend my viewpoint.

Materials: Paper and pen or computer or Google Documents; the students' lists from 3.5.

The students will use the lists generated in 3.5. They will divide into pairs. Each student will present one side of the argument, followed by the next student presenting the opposing side. The students will also decide on time limits and rules for debating.

3.7 I can offer constructive criticism in a kind manner.

Materials: Handouts pertaining to constructive criticism (Appendix B, pp. 75-76).

The teacher/leader will distribute the handouts. Students will write responses to the various situations and/or students will role play the part of the leader who must offer constructive criticism. The students will critique each others' reactions to the situations presented. The students will create their own infographic, outlining the do's and don'ts of constructive criticism.

3.8 I know the various types of speeches and when each should be used.

Materials: Paper and pen or computers or Google Documents.

The students will generate a list of various types of speeches and discuss when they should be used (Appendix B, p. 76). Small excerpts from famous speeches or transcripts of certain speeches are helpful here. The students will then select one type of speech to prepare and present.

3.9 I can deliver a prepared speech to a group.

Materials: Speeches prepared in 3.8.

The students will give the speeches they have prepared in 3.8.

3.10 I can deliver an extemporaneous speech to a group.

Materials: Speech topics written on slips of paper.

The teacher/leader will generate topics pertinent to student interest and will place them in a hat or box. Each student will select a topic from the hat or box and give a three-minute extemporaneous speech. The students not giving the speech will critique. Students giving the speeches will review the feedback as soon as possible.

3.11 I can moderate and direct panel discussions.

Materials: None required.

The students will select topics from those suggested in one of the above activities (3.5, 3.10) and divide into groups to form panels. They will research the topics, elect a leader, and present their panel discussions. Students will receive anonymous feedback to each panel discussion from the other students watching the panel discussion.

3.12 I listen carefully to others in order to be an effective communicator.

Materials: None required.

The students will divide into pairs and listen to each other describe some important event, celebration, disappointment, etc. The person listening will then repeat all of the details that they can remember. Students will then discuss which listening techniques helped them to remember the most.

3.13 I can use body language effectively as I speak.

Materials: Checklist of body language (Appendix B, p. 77); film or videotape.

The students will view a film or videotape that the teacher has selected with the sound turned off. They will then discuss the various methods of body language used. The students will be given a checklist of body language at the beginning of this section. Each time they listen to a student speaker, they will use this checklist and give their results to the speaker.

3.14 I am honest and sincere when speaking.

Materials: White Board and markers; paper and pen; computers; Google Documents.

The students will brainstorm ways in which people portray honesty and sincerity. They will also list ways to spot an insincere person.

Character-Building Skills (CBS)

4.1 I understand my own feelings.

Materials: Worksheet with appropriate headings.

The teacher will distribute a worksheet with such headings as "sad," "happy," "angry," "homesick," etc. and have the students list personal experiences under the appropriate headings. The teacher may also use unfinished sentences such as, "I am happy when...." The students will share those experiences they feel comfortable discussing.

4.2 I care about others and treat others fairly.

Materials: Paper and pen or computers or Google Documents.

As a group, students will brainstorm "fairness" in our world. What is "fairness"? What does it look like to be "fair"? The students will choose four people that they care about and list ways in which they could show "fairness" towards them.

The teacher will lead a discussion on the importance of treating all persons in a "fair" manner.

4.3 I try to understand the feelings of others.

Materials: None required.

The teacher/leader will choose one pupil to portray the role of a school leader who has had to make a decision that will impact different people in various ways. Other students will portray the people whose lives are affected. The remaining students will critique the manner in which students portray their feelings and the way in which the leader responds to them. Students will trade roles periodically.

Suggested topics for these situations are: competitive sports are eliminated; the band will no longer be funded by the school board; the annual dance has been cancelled, etc.

4.4 I am sensitive to the needs of others.

Materials: Cards with personality types on them (Appendix B, p. 78).

The teacher will appoint one student to play the part of a leader attempting to conduct a meeting. The teacher will then distribute cards to other students who will role play the personality type described on the card. At the end of 10 minutes, the class will discuss the needs of each based on the personality types they have observed and how each can be dealt with effectively.

4.5 I am sincere in my interest in other people.

Materials: Dictionary; White Board and markers; dictionary.

The teacher/leader will ask for definitions of "manipulation" and will write them on the board. One student will look up the definition in the dictionary and will lead a discussion on the difference between "interest" and "manipulation."

4.6 I try to deal honestly with others.

Materials: Paper and pen; computer; Google Documents; White Board and markers.

The teacher/leader will record various occupations that the students suggest and lead a discussion about the role of ethics in each field. The teacher/leader will also pose the problem of how to deal with unethical people or actions which will also be followed by discussion time.

4.7 I do what I say I will do.

Materials: Paper and pen or computer or Google Documents or White board and markers.

The students will discuss task-commitment. They will also focus on the dangers of the over-extended leader and on how to deal with people who don't follow through by doing what they say they will. The teacher/leader asks students to generate examples of commitment and over-extension.

4.8 I have strong beliefs and can defend them when necessary.

Materials: Paper and pen or computer or Google Documents.

The students will get together in groups to develop a role-playing situation in which a leader's values are attacked and he/she is called on to defend them.

The students will engage in a discussion of how well they know their own personal values.

4.9 I am willing to admit my mistakes.

Materials: Cards portraying appropriate and inappropriate ways of admitting mistakes to others (Appendix B, p. 78).

The teacher/leader will distribute the cards and ask the students to react to them by stating if they are appropriate or inappropriate. If the latter is the case, the students will be asked to state a way in which the situation could be changed.

The students will then discuss other appropriate ways to admit mistakes and inappropriate ways to do the same.

4.10 I have a set of personal standards.

Materials: None required.

The leader will brainstorm with the group in order to establish a definition of "personal standards". A discussion should follow focusing on the difficulty of maintaining "personal standards" when faced with peer pressure.

The students will think of examples from history and literature of persons who have upheld their "personal standards"

4.11 I have free choice in establishing my values.

Materials: None required.

The students will divide into groups of three and discuss the role of influence in their lives. They will examine how much their values have been affected by others and the point at which they began to think for themselves.

4.12 I know the things in my life that are important to me.

Materials: Handout "Values in My Life" (Appendix B, p. 79).

The teacher/leader will distribute the handout and the students will be given 5-10 minutes to complete it. They will then discuss their choices.

4.13 I can state my choices publicly.

Materials: Editorials from several different newspapers; paper and pen or computer.

The students will read the editorials and comment upon the values that are expressed. They will then write their own editorials expressing their viewpoints on a current issue.

4.14 I can keep my own standards, even when others disagree with me.

Materials: Editorials from 4.13.

The students will exchange editorials and write rebuttals. They will discuss the following questions: How tenaciously should someone maintain his/her position? Is it a weakness in a leader if his/her viewpoint changes?

4.15 I can accept other people's ideas and choices, even when they are different from mine.

Materials: A list of various cultural, ethnic, and religious groups established by the teacher/leader and students.

The students will discuss how the way of life and beliefs of various groups differ. They will consider the question: How well has America and the world managed to accommodate so many divergent views, and beliefs, and ways of life?

4.16 I respect the rights of others.

Materials: White Board and markers or paper and pen or computer or Google Slides.

The teacher/leader will instruct the students to pretend that they are the leader of their local student council. As a leader, what rights of the individual must they protect?

The lists generated will be compared and discussed by the class.

4.17 I am loyal to my superiors and my friends.

Materials: None required.

The teacher/leader will lead a discussion on loyalty and its meaning. The teacher/leader should cite instances from history that will serve to illustrate this concept.

Decision-Making Skills (DMS)

5.1 I understand decision-making skills.

Materials: White Board and markers or paper and pen or computer or Google Documents.

The teacher will ask students to reflect on a recent decision they have made which has affected their lives in some way. The students will write down the steps they went through in making the decision. They will compare the steps when all are finished.

5.2 I can gather facts for decision-making.

Materials: Handout "Susan and her Decision" (Appendix B, p. 80); pen and paper or computer.

The teacher may generate his/her own scenario if desired, or students may make suggestions within a leadership situation.

The teacher reads the scenario and asks the students to make four columns on their papers titled: "Things to Think About;" "People to Talk To;" "Things to Read;" and "Things to Do." The students will list, under each, person or thing where they can gather facts.

5.3 I can accept advice from others.

Materials: Lists from 5.2.

The teacher/leader will instruct students to put a check by the three people on the list who could help them the most. Each student will tell who the most influential person would be and why.

5.4 I can analyze facts before making a decision.

Materials: Lists from 5.2.

The students will discuss materials they listed to read and places they would visit to gather facts. They will also answer the following questions: How should Susan weigh these facts? Which sources and places would have the most accurate and up-to-date information? What part do feelings play in all of this?

5.5 I am aware of how my decisions will affect others.

Materials: Lists from 5.2; White Board and makers or computer or Google documents.

The teacher/leader will ask the students the following questions: What people will be affected by Susan's decision? How important are each of these people to her? How will Susan deal with each of these individuals? The students will respond orally. The teacher/leader will then compile lists on the White Board or computer.

5.6 I know how to reach logical conclusions.

Materials: Handout "A Critical Decision" (Appendix B, p. 80).

The students will read the scenario and discuss the logic or lack of it in each suggestion that is offered.

5.7 I can reach decisions on my own.

Materials: Paper and pen or computer or Google Documents.

The teacher/leader will instruct the students to make a list of people who have had a strong influence on them. The students will rate each person according to the amount of influence that they have over them. They will then discuss whether this influence is positive or negative.

5.8 I can make a decision quickly and accurately based on facts.

Materials: White Board and markers or computers or Google Documents.

The students will discuss impulsive personalities versus reflective personalities and answer the following questions: What are the pros and cons of each? How quickly should decisions be made? How can you assess the risk-taking factors of decisions?

5.9 I can accept the fact that my decisions may not always be popular in my group.

Materials: None required.

The teacher/leader will pose the following questions: How would you react to being ostracized by members of your peer group? How would you handle a situation in which you had to make a very unpopular decision? Teachers/leaders and students will generate a situation in which an unpopular decision has been made and role play the various people involved.

5.10 I can support group decisions, even though I do not always agree with them.

Materials: None required.

The teacher/leader will continue the discussion for 5.9, but will pose these new problems:

a. How do I react when the group reaches a decision with which I do not agree?

b. How do I live with this?

c. What are my alternatives?

d. Should I resign?

Group Dynamic Skills (GDS)

6.1 I can lead a group discussion.

Materials: Paper and pen or computer or Google Documents.

The students will prepare a topic for a group discussion and will write down probing questions that could be used to move the discussion along. They will take turns introducing their topics and leading a short discussion (5 minutes).

6.2 I enjoy group activities.

Materials: Paper and pen; White Board and markers; computers; or Google Documents.

The teacher/leader will lead the students in a discussion of types of group activities they most enjoy. Students will compile their own lists and rate the activities according to those they feel most adequate to lead.

6.3 I know what "brainstorming" is and can lead a group in this exercise.

Materials: Handout "Brainstorming" (Appendix B, p. 81).

The teacher/leader will go over the purpose and the rules for brainstorming with the students and will ask for suggestions of occasions when brainstorming would be an appropriate activity. Students will practice conducting such sessions.

6.4 I can use parliamentary procedure in leading a group.

Materials: Handout on parliamentary procedure (Appendix B, p. 81).

The teacher will discuss with the students the important points of parliamentary procedure, the reasons for it, and when it is appropriate to use it. The students will set up a "mock meeting" demonstrating the correct use of parliamentary procedure.

6.5 I use "we" instead of "I" when conducting group sessions on matters that involve the group.

Materials: None required.

The teacher/leader will lead a discussion on the importance of group cohesiveness and the leader's responsibility in developing it. The students will examine the use of "we" instead of "I."

6.6 I can lead a group so that people feel safe expressing their opinions.

Materials: None required.

The class will discuss the fact that the leader sets the tone for a meeting. The students will brainstorm ways, both verbal and non-verbal, in which a leader can help individuals feel safe in expressing their opinions.

6.7 I usually allow others to express their opinions before I express mine.

Materials: White Board and markers or computer or Google Documents.

The students will conduct a discussion focusing on the "etiquette" of being a good leader. One student will serve as recorder and make a list of suggestions on the White Board or on a computer.

6.8 I try to understand the viewpoints of others.

Materials: Handout "The Student Council" (Appendix B, p. 82).

The students will read the scenario and attempt to describe each individual's differing point of view and why it is valid. They will discuss what the leader of the group could do in this situation.

6.9 I keep in mind the best interests of the group.

Materials: Scenario from 6.8.

The students will discuss what they feel would truly be in the best interest of the group in the above situations. The pros and cons of each position will be explored.

6.10 I can resolve conflicts within a group.

Materials: Scenario from 6.8; paper and pen or computer; or Google Documents.

The students will now attempt to bring about the resolution of the conflict in a manner that would be most fair and most equitable to all. Each student will outline his/her own plan of action privately and then discuss this with the group.

6.11 I recognize and value differences in individuals.

Materials: Cards with personality types on them (used in 4.4; see Appendix B, p. 78).

The students will review the various personality types presented previously and discuss how an effective leader could incorporate the traits of each type in group situations.

6.12 I can distinguish between influence and manipulation.

Materials: Dictionary; White Board and markers or computer or Google Documents.

The teacher/leader will ask one student to look up the terms "lobby" and "lobbyist" and to write the definitions on the board. They will then lead a discussion on the role of influence and how it differs from manipulation.

6.13 I do not take it personally when others disagree with my ideas.

Materials: "Objectivity" written on the White Board or paper and pen or computer.

The students will discuss ways in which they can become more objective about themselves in order to become better leaders. The teacher/leader will pose the question, "How do you deal with hurt feelings?" The students will then develop their own personal strategies for dealing with their own objectivity and their own feelings.

6.14 I can maintain trust within a group.

Materials: "Trust" written on the White Board and markers or paper and pen or computer or Google Documents.

The students will divide into groups of four or five and discuss the term "trust." They will compile a list of ways that a leader can maintain trust within a group. The small groups will come back together and compare lists.

6.15 I can keep a group on task.

Materials: Handout "A Task to Be Accomplished" (Appendix B, p. 82); paper and pen; computer or Google Documents.

The students will read the handout and then construct a plan of action in which they will show a timeline, how they would delegate authority as the leader, and how they would check on progress.

6.16 I can incorporate the suggestions of others.

Materials: Plans from 6.15.

The students will share with the group their plans developed in 6.15. Fellow students will offer suggestions, and the presenter will respond by either incorporating the suggestions, modifying them, or rejecting them. They must give a rationale for each decision.

6.17 I can work effectively for compromise.

Materials: Computer for research

The teacher/leader will lead a discussion on "the art of compromise" and its importance in leadership and diplomacy. The students will cite examples from history in which compromise played a key role in a leadership situation.

6.18 I can help the group agree upon a plan of action.

Materials: Paper and pen or computer or Google Documents.

The students will plan a culminating activity for the end of the leadership class or workshop. They will draw up a plan for leadership, delegate responsibility, and set a timeline.

6.19 I can give credit and praise to others for work well done.

Materials: Paper and pen or computer or Google Documents.

The students will each take a sheet of paper with the heading "Positive Reinforcement" and brainstorm ways in which people can be given credit and praise for work well done. The students will individually rank the suggestions according to their own priorities. Students will role play giving positive reinforcement to others.

Problem-Solving Skills (PSS)

7.1 I know and use the elements of problem-solving.

Materials: Handout "Steps for Solving Problems" (Appendix B, p. 83).

The teacher/leader will go through the steps presented in the handout, discussing each thoroughly. Each student will come up with a problem and use the technique that they have just learned to formulate a plan of action.

7.2 I know what to do as a leader in problem-solving situations.

Materials: None required.

The students will simulate a club meeting. They will work in pairs to formulate a problem that is facing the group. The student pairs will lead the rest of the group in working out solutions to their proposed problems.

7.3 I can identify present and potential problems.

Materials: White Board and markers or paper and pen or computer or Google Documents.

The students will brainstorm problems facing their country, community, and/or school. Problems will be listed and prioritized.

7.4 I can develop different ways to solve problems.

Materials: Lists compiled in 7.3.

The students will divide into groups and try to generate creative ways to solve some of these problems.

7.5 I can select the best way to solve a problem.

Materials: Solutions generated in 7.4.

The students will decide which of the solutions proposed in 7.4 is the best solution based on personnel available, economic factors, and other major resources.

7.6 I can evaluate how effective my problem-solving strategies are.

Materials: The solution compiled from 7.5.

The students will develop strategies to evaluate and judge the effectiveness of their solution. The students will then list their own problems and outline the steps that they will use to solve them.

Personal Skills (PERS)

8.1 I am self-confident.

Materials: "I am good at..." written on the White Board, computer or with pen and paper.

The students will list things which they feel best complete the statement. They will establish goals for things they would like to do better, relating these to leadership.

8.2 I feel comfortable in most situations.

Materials: White Board and markers or paper and pen or computer or Google Documents.

The students will brainstorm situations in which they feel uncomfortable. They will role play some of the situations, demonstrating appropriate and inappropriate behavior. The students will then list situations in which they feel the most comfortable and the reasons why, discussing how any of these situations relate to leadership.

8.3 I can identify my own strengths and weaknesses.

Materials: Paper and pen or computer or Google Documents.

The students will make a list of personal strengths and rank them. They will discuss how each personal strength will make them a better leader.

8.4 I can acknowledge my mistakes.

Materials: None required.

The students will discuss the biggest mistakes they have ever made. They will then demonstrate how these situations should have been handled. The teacher/leader will pose the questions: Why is it important to make mistakes? Why is the ability to admit mistakes important to a leader?

8.5 I can accept constructive criticism.

Materials: None required.

The teacher/leader will discuss the value of receiving constructive criticism in light of personal growth and development. The students will discuss why it is important to seek constructive criticism, especially for a leader. They will then break into pairs and give and receive constructive criticism on personal skills.8.6 I actively strive toward self-improvement.

Materials: Paper and pen or computer or Google Documents.

The students should make a list of those areas of their lives needing self-improvement. Areas would include academic, social, emotional, etc. Each student will develop a self-improvement plan with timelines.

A discussion will follow focusing on how these self-improvements will aid leadership ability.

8.7 I am persistent.

Materials: None required.

The teacher/leader will pose the questions: What obstacles do you find the hardest to overcome as a leader? What things are discouraging to you? How do you deal with these? A discussion will follow.

8.8 I try to avoid negatively internalizing constructive criticism by striving to process my emotions in an objective manner.

Materials: Paper and pen or computers or Google Documents.

The teacher/leader will have students talk about how they felt when they were on the receiving end of activity 8.5, in which they listened to constructive criticism about themselves. The students will discuss ways of handling feelings in a more objective manner and list reasons why this skill is important for leaders.

8.9 I strive to be punctual and on time.

Materials: None required.

The teacher/leader will lead a discussion on the reasons (i.e., attention or power) that people are late. The students will then develop strategies for arriving at places on time. They will consider the question: How does promptness or tardiness affect people's perceptions of a leader?

8.10 I am reliable.

Materials: Paper and pen, computers, or Google Documents.

The students will list ways to indicate that they are reliable. The teacher/leader will lead a discussion on how reliability affects others' opinions of a leader.

8.11 I am enthusiastic.

Materials: None required.

The teacher/leader will lead a discussion of how a group mirrors the mood of its leader. "Enthusiasm is Contagious" will be the theme.

8.12 I am ambitious and desire success.

Materials: None required.

The group will discuss how the self-confident person views success. They will also discuss the ethics of success. The teacher/leader will pose the questions: Are all leaders success-oriented? How important is this quality to a leader?

8.13 I am competent and a hard worker.

Materials: Paper and pen, computers, or Google Documents.

The students take a blank sheet of paper with the heading "The Price of Success" and will brainstorm what they might have to give up in order to be a successful leader. They will also discuss the difference between working "hard" and working "smart."

8.14 I can understand and deal with abstract concepts.

Materials: "Am I an Idea Person or an Action Person?" written on the White Board.

The students will think about the question as it concerns themselves. They will then discuss how important each trait (ideas versus actions) is in a leader.

8.15 I am patient with myself and others.

Materials: None required.

The students will divide into small groups and share with each other their concepts of "realistic expectations," both concerning themselves and others and how this trait could affect one's leadership ability.

8.16 I make friends easily.

Materials: None required.

The students will brainstorm and discuss the qualities they value in a friend. They will also discuss the idea that the very qualities that make them leaders may also cause envy in others.

8.17 I try to be thoughtful about the feelings of others.

Materials: Handout "Difficult Situations" (Appendix B, p. 83).

The students will draw slips and role play various difficult situations showing how they, as leaders, could handle them in a sensitive manner.

8.18 I make an effort to remember names and faces.

Materials: None required.

The teacher/leader will discuss the importance of using people's names when addressing them. The group will discuss methods to aid in remembering people's names and how important this is to a leader. Students may rename themselves and have the class attempt to remember their new names.

8.19 I can get along with others.

Materials: None required.

The students will discuss how important diplomacy is for a leader. They will also discuss and role play how they can make others feel like an integral part of a group.

8.20 I know how to dress for different occasions.

Materials: Pictures cut from magazines supplied by the teacher/leader or students.

The students will discuss the occasions for which each person in the pictures is appropriately dressed. They will discuss the phrase "Dress for Success" and its implications in leadership.

8.21 I am neat and appropriate in my work and appearance.

Materials: None required.

The teacher/leader will lead a discussion on the importance of neatness and how this reflects on the individual, as well as on the group that the person represents as a leader.

Planning Skills (PS)

9.1 I have organizational skills.

Materials: Checklist of planning skills (Appendix B, p. 84).

The teacher will distribute the checklist of planning skills, and the students will evaluate themselves.

9.2 I set achievable goals for myself.

Materials: Paper and pen, computers, or Google Documents.

After a discussion on the difference between goals and objectives, each student will set one goal that he/she will accomplish in 24 hours, in one week, in one month, and in one year. The students will discuss in small groups how realistic their goals are.

9.3 I set achievable goals for groups.

Materials: White Board and markers, computer, or Google Documents.

The students will brainstorm goals that they wish to accomplish as a group during this leadership training program.

9.4 I can take the lead in group planning.

Materials: The students' list of goals that they hope to accomplish from 9.3.

The students will divide into small groups. Each will take a turn as leader, presenting their ideas and leading the group planning session.

9.5 I can accept suggestions from other people.

Materials: Plans made in 9.4.

The students will discuss how they felt when people disagreed with their ideas. Each will cite one good suggestion that they received from someone else.

9.6 I can direct the efforts of the group.

Materials: None required.

The students will discuss the ease or difficulty that they experienced in leading the planning groups in activity 9.4.

9.7 I seek advice when necessary.

Materials: Paper and pen or computer or Google Documents.

The students will list several major headings: academic, financial, religious, political, etc. They will then list under each heading the people they would turn to for advice.

9.8 I can set objectives to help accomplish my goals.

Materials: Personal goals from 9.2.

The students will outline objectives to help accomplish the goals set in activity 9.2.

9.9 I can anticipate and/or predict the outcomes of certain actions.

Materials: None required.

The teacher/leader will lead a discussion on the importance of thinking ahead and the consequences of not doing so.

9.10 I can determine what is needed to accomplish certain goals.

Materials: Strategies outlined in 9.8.

The students will make a list of resources needed to accomplish their goals.

9.11 I can develop and keep to a timeline.

Materials: Personal goals from 9.2; strategies from 9.8., pen and paper or computer

The students will choose one of their long-term goals with the accompanying strategies and will develop a timeline.

9.12 I can meet deadlines.

Materials: None required.

The students will discuss the importance of responsibility and how meeting deadlines is part of a person's responsibility as a leader. They will brainstorm suggestions for helping people to meet deadlines.

9.13 I can set up ways to measure whether or not my goals are completed.

Materials: Timelines from 9.11, pen and paper or computer.

The students will develop evaluation strategies to coincide with their timelines.

9.14 I am not overwhelmed by details.

Materials: None required.

The students will discuss how leaders can help to avoid being overwhelmed by details. They will also discuss delegating authority.

9.15 I am flexible and can accept change.

Materials: None required.

The students will divide into small groups and discuss flexibility and their own tolerance for change. They may also wish to discuss the consequences of being inflexible.

9.16 I can delegate authority to others.

Materials: Paper and pencil or computer or Google Documents.

The students will review the plans that they have made in the previous activities and list which responsibilities could be delegated to other people. Discussion should follow on factors to be considered in delegating authority, such as personalities, the ability to lead groups, skill for certain tasks, the amount of time available, etc.

17 I review my plans and revise them when necessary.

Materials: Timelines from 9.11; handout "Plan for Leadership" (Appendix B, p. 85), pen and paper or computer.

The students will mark checkpoints on their timelines at which they will review their strategies and revise them if necessary.

At this point, the students are instructed in designing and implementing a "Plan for Leadership." They will select one long-range realistic goal focusing on leadership and develop a plan of action using the steps outlined above. The plan should take no longer than six to 12 months to complete, and it should have a positive impact. The students may want to initiate or change something in their school, community, or religious affiliation.

Appendix A: Samples Used in Developing the LSI

Table 1: Means, Standard Deviations, and Internal Consistency Coefficients for the Total Sample (N=452)

	n	X	SD	Split Half	Kuder Richardson	Spearman Brown
Fundamentals of Leadership	9	19.84	4.21	.81	.78	.80
Written Communication Skills	12	23.76	7.70	.84	.83	.84
Speech Communication Skills	14	25.84	8.41	.85	.84	.85
Character-Building Skills	17	38.65	10.09	.89	.86	.89
Decision-Making Skills	10	21.20	6.35	.85	.83	.85
Group Dynamic Skills	19	37.60	11.94	.92	.90	.93
Problem-Solving Skills	6	11.80	3.94	.83	.81	.83
Personal Skills	21	46.79	12.47	.91	.88	.91
Planning Skills	17	32.86	10.55	.90	.89	.90

Table 2: Means, Standard Deviations, and Internal Consistency Coefficients for the Total Sample (N=56)

	n	X	SD	Split Half	Kuder Richardson	Spearman Brown
Fundamentals of Leadership	9	20.88	3.53	.75	.72	.77
Written Communication Skills	12	26.20	4.92	.80	.77	.80
Speech Communication Skills	14	27.09	6.31	.91	.85	.91
Character-Building Skills	17	43.09	4.93	.85	.83	.85
Decision-Making Skills	10	22.71	3.07	.80	.70	.80
Group Dynamic Skills	19	41.43	6.94	.88	.84	.88
Problem-Solving Skills	6	11.84	2.77	.87	.84	.87
Personal Skills	21	49.63	6.30	.81	.79	.82
Planning Skills	17	35.29	6.52	.85	.83	.85

Table 3: Means, Standard Deviations, and Internal Consistency Coefficients for the Total Sample (N=59)

	n	X	SD	Split Half	Kuder Richardson	Spearman Brown
Fundamentals of Leadership	9	24.02	3.28	.73	.72	.74
Written Communication Skills	12	27.73	4.90	.80	.82	.80
Speech Communication Skills	14	30.17	5.29	.85	.79	.86
Character-Building Skills	17	43.46	4..39	.82	.79	.83
Decision-Making Skills	10	23.71	3.48	.84	.79	.85
Group Dynamic Skills	19	44.34	6.89	.90	.87	.91
Problem-Solving Skills	6	13.36	2.60	.78	.77	.79
Personal Skills	21	53.14	5.68	.89	.82	.89
Planning Skills	17	38.80	6.35	.88	.86	.88

Table 4: Means, Standard Deviations, and Internal Consistency Coefficients for the Total Sample (N=27)

	n	X	SD	Split Half	Kuder Richardson	Spearman Brown
Fundamentals of Leadership	9	18.85	3.03	.65	.65	.56
Written Communication Skills	12	24.26	6.16	.82	.82	.85
Speech Communication Skills	14	25.11	6.62	.93	.93	.90
Character-Building Skills	17	40.04	7.00	.83	.84	.84
Decision-Making Skills	10	22.48	7.93	.87	.87	.89
Group Dynamic Skills	19	38.19	10.86	.95	.95	.93
Problem-Solving Skills	6	11.63	3.60	.92	.94	.89
Personal Skills	21	50.48	9.12	.87	.87	.91
Planning Skills	17	31.70	9.96	.94	.94	.91

Table 5: Means standard deviations and coefficients of stability for a Louisiana sample(N=45)

	N	X	Sd	Test retest (4 weeks)
Fundamentals of Leadership	9	20.16	3.89	.30
Written Communication Skills	12	23.79	5.70	.62
Speech Communication Skills	14	26.13	6.36	.67
Character Building Skills	17	39.40	6.07	.64
Descision Making Skills	10	22.02	4.32	.48
Group Dynamic Skills	19	39.32	8.31	.49
Problem Solving Skills	6	13.08	3.29	.42
Personal Skills	21	48.59	7.72	.32
Planning Skills	17	35.41	7.25	.37

Table 6: Means, Standard Deviations, and Internal Consistency Coefficients for the Total Sample (N=107)

	n	X	SD	Split Half	Kuder Richardson	Spearman Brown
Fundamentals of Leadership	9	19.31	4.54	.78	.77	.78
Written Communication Skills	12	23.79	6.48	.86	.81	.81
Speech Communication Skills	14	26.73	7.46	.84	.84	.83
Character-Building Skills	17	39.17	7.44	.90	.88	.90
Decision-Making Skills	10	21.39	5.11	.88	.85	.88
Group Dynamic Skills	19	37.21	10.92	.93	.92	.93
Problem-Solving Skills	6	12.27	3.22	.84	.80	.84
Personal Skills	21	47.29	8.94	.94	.89	.94
Planning Skills	17	32.92	9.34	.91	.91	.91

Table 7: Means, Standard Deviations, and Internal Consistency Coefficients for the Total Sample (N=75)

	n	X	SD	Split Half	Kuder Richardson	Spearman Brown
Fundamentals of Leadership	9	18.60	.4.75	.79	.74	.79
Written Communication Skills	12	23.57	6.87	.91	.86	.92
Speech Communication Skills	14	25.20	6.42	.85	.79	.84
Character-Building Skills	17	38.43	6.81	.86	.83	.86
Decision-Making Skills	10	20.85	4.86	.84	.78	.85
Group Dynamic Skills	19	36.00	9.22	.91	.88	.91
Problem-Solving Skills	6	11.11	3.25	.80	.76	.80
Personal Skills	21	45.73	9.79	.91	.89	.92
Planning Skills	17	30.85	8.68	.89	.87	.89

Table 8: Means, Standard Deviations, and Internal Consistency Coefficients` for the Total Sample (N=24)

	n	X	SD	Split Half	Kuder Richardson	Spearman Brown
Fundamentals of Leadership	9	20.33	3.67	.65	.69	.67
Written Communication Skills	12	25.67	6.14	.74	.78	.74
Speech Communication Skills	14	30.13	6.31	.67	.78	.67
Character-Building Skills	17	40.89	6.92	.86	.85	.87
Decision-Making Skills	10	22.86	4.65	.78	.86	.79
Group Dynamic Skills	19	42.04	7.92	.94	.89	.94
Problem-Solving Skills	6	12.33	3.00	.69	.71	.72
Personal Skills	21	51.75	5.42	.89	.90	.91
Planning Skills	17	36.33	6.45	.93	.90	.95

Table 9: Means, Standard Deviations, and Internal Consistency Coefficients for the Total Sample (N=59)

	n	X	SD	Split Half	Kuder Richardson	Spearman Brown
Fundamentals of Leadership	9	21.19	4.03	.90	.85	.91
Written Communication Skills	12	20.56	13.71	.88	.88	.88
Speech Communication Skills	14	22.02	14.74	.85	.86	.85
Character-Building Skills	17	31.08	20.25	.91	.87	.91
Decision-Making Skills	10	17.33	11.47	.88	.83	.88
Group Dynamic Skills	19	31.98	21.35	.95	.92	.95
Problem-Solving Skills	6	9.69	6.59	.85	.82	.86
Personal Skills	21	38.05	24.82	.95	.89	.95
Planning Skills	17	28.33	18.79	.87	.90	.88

Appendix B: Supplementary Materials for the Leadership Instructional Activities

(This Appendix may be duplicated for classroom use only.)

Leadership Styles (1.4)

Laissez Faire—This style of leadership is characterized by non-interference with the affairs of the group. The leader exercises minimum control and influence over the followers but is available to group members as an adviser.

Democratic—This style of leadership is characterized by an adherence to parliamentary procedure. The leader functions as a member of the group in many instances. The chief leadership function is to emphasize the will of the group.

Authoritarian—This style of leadership is characterized by absolute adherence to authority. The leader makes all major plans and decisions. This individual alone directs all activities of the group. This is a very ego-centered leadership style.

Problem Situations (1.5)

1. You are editor of the school newspaper. In the beginning of the year, your staff members were all "eager beavers". However, it is now mid-term. Staff members are failing to hand in assignments on time, and in some cases, not at all. What could you do to motivate them?
2. You are chairperson of a fund-raising activity. Your committee members have really worked hard and have reached their goal several weeks ahead of schedule. What would you say to them at the next meeting?
3. You have just been elected President of the Student Council. One of your main objectives is to restructure the council and make it more effective. How should you proceed?
4. You have been appointed to head an important school committee because the previous chairperson has moved out of town. The committee is overdue in meeting its objectives and doesn't appear to be clear on its goals. People have stopped coming to meetings, and those who do come only want to talk and socialize. As the leader, what can you do?

Sources of Information (2.1)

- Almanacs
- Annuals
- Anthologies
- Archives
- Atlases
- Audiotapes
- Books
- Brochures
- Computers
- Diaries
- Dictionaries
- Directories
- Documents (Government, Business, Historical, etc.)
- DVDs
- Encyclopedias
- Filmstrips
- Globes
- Handbooks
- Indexes
- Internet (World Wide Web)
- Manuals
- Maps
- Microfiche
- Microfilm
- Monographs
- Movies
- Newspapers
- Pamphlets
- Periodicals
- Records
- Resource Persons
- Reviews
- Slides
- Software
- Television
- Thesauri
- Videotapes

Parts of a Business Letter (2.8)

Heading
Inside Address
Salutation
Body of the Letter
Complimentary Close
Signature

Sample Business Letter (2.8)

909 South 38th Avenue
Blueville, Mississippi 87248
Date

Mayor Lawrence West
City Office Building
114 Blueville Street
Blueville, MS 87248

Dear Mayor West:

Leadership is a very important skill to have. Because of this, the Juniors at Blueville High School are studying the many components of leadership. We would like to hear your views on leadership. Would you consider speaking to our group on December 15?

Sincerely yours,

Betty Butler

Sample Social Letter (2.9)

909 South 38th Avenue
Blueville, Mississippi 87248
Date

Dear Mayor West,

Thank you for your very interesting talk on leadership. The ideas and suggestions will be of great value to me as we continue our study of leadership.

Sincerely yours,

Betty Butler

Sample Agenda (2.10)

Call to Order.

"The meeting will now come to order." If guests are present, they should be recognized.

Additional Agenda Items.

"Are there additional agenda items?" Place the new items under either new business or unfinished business.

Reading of the Minutes.

"The Secretary will read the minutes of the last meeting."
"Are there any deletions, additions, or corrections?"
If not, "The minutes are approved as read," or if so, "The minutes are approved as corrected."

Treasurer's Report.

(Same as above.)

Reports of Other Officers and Committees.

Unfinished Business.

New Business.

Program.

Not all meetings will involve a program. If there is a program, introduce the speaker.

Announcements.

"Are there any announcements?" or "The following announcements should be made."

Adjournment.

"Is there a motion that the meeting be adjourned?"
"Is there a second?"
"The meeting is adjourned."

How to Give Constructive Criticism (3.7)

Whenever two or more people live and/or work together, it is inevitable that some disagreement will arise from time to time. It is usually incumbent upon the leader to settle such disagreements. Another function of leadership is to evaluate the performance of others. This calls for special skills. In both of these circumstances, the ability to give constructive criticism is required.

There are ways to handle these situations tactfully and constructively. Here are some general principles which, when mastered, can help to reduce the negative impact of what we must say or do.

1. Always be well prepared. Think out or plan in advance what behavior it is that you want to improve.
2. Be specific. Get to the point quickly. Do not keep the other person guessing or wondering about what it is you have to say.
3. Talk about the person's performance or behavior, but do not criticize the person. This will reduce defensiveness and hurt feelings.
4. Use "I" statements. This allows you to express the conflict as your own. "I was upset when I discovered that the minutes were not ready." "When people are late for meetings, I get annoyed by the delays."
5. Listen carefully to what the person has to say in response. There are always two sides to every story. Be prepared to acknowledge a mistake, if there is one.
6. Be specific about how you want behavior to change. Sometimes this requires negotiation on the part of all people concerned. Be prepared to give a little.
7. If you feel that the situation warrants it, be prepared to discuss the consequences of continuing the undesirable behavior.
8. Be sure, before you separate, that everyone clearly understands what has been discussed and agreed upon.
9. Take time to show appreciation. Giving, or especially receiving, criticism, even when it is constructive, is not pleasant. Focusing on the positive aspects of the relationship can bring people closer together after they have worked through difficulties.

Sample Situations of Constructive Criticism (3.7)

1. The president of a club is acutely aware of the fact that one of the officers tends to monopolize the conversation in almost all meetings. Several people have complained, and attendance is dropping off at the meetings.
2. One of the students at your school has submitted an essay for publication in the school's literary magazine. The essay contains many statements that could cause hurt and discomfort to other students. The editor feels that they must meet with the student to offer suggestions for revising the essay.
3. The treasurer of a school organization has been very remiss about collecting dues and giving an accurate financial report at every meeting. The president of the organization knows that he/she needs to do something about this situation.
4. The secretary of a club has turned in minutes that are inaccurate, contain misspelled words, and are generally rather sloppy. The president knows something must be done soon.
5. The chairperson of the local computer club worked diligently to establish the organization. However, they did not plan an agenda for the meetings, nor did they begin and end them on time.

Types of Speeches (3.8)

- ❍ Nominating
- ❍ Congratulatory
- ❍ Extemporaneous
- ❍ Point of View
- ❍ Introductory
- ❍ Persuasive
- ❍ Humorous
- ❍ Illustrative or Demonstrative
- ❍ Rebuttal

Checklist of Body Language (3.13)

Mark each item with a plus (+) or minus (-).

Head

____1. Held erect
____2. Moves to emphasize a point and maintains eye contact

Eyes

____1. Expressive
____2. Meets eyes of audience
____3. Focuses on entire group

Hands

____1. Uses for emphasis
____2. Elbows slightly bent
____3. Gestures appropriate
____4. Relaxed
____5. Does not fidget

Torso

____1. Good posture
____2. Erect
____3. Comfortable

Feet

____1. Good balance
____2. Slightly apart
____3. When sitting, slightly bent, ankles crossed

Overall

____1. Sincere
____2. Animated
____3. Confident
____4. Enthusiastic
____5. Friendly
____6. Good communicator

COMMENTS:

Suggested Personality Types (4.4)

Class Clown—a person who jokes and acts out

Obnoxious—a person who is loud, boring, over-opinionated

Manipulative—a person who tries to get people to do what he/she wants by using sneaky methods

Extrovert—a person who is outgoing, friendly, talkative

Introvert—a person who is shy, speaks very little, does not stand out in a group

Expert—a person who knows it all, brags, puts everyone else down

Dictator—a person who does not want to listen to anyone else's opinion

Conciliatory—a person who tries to make peace and smooth things over

Suggested Appropriate and Inappropriate Ways of Admitting Mistakes (4.9)

- ❍ I'm sorry that I didn't keep to a good time schedule and that the project isn't finished.
- ❍ Jean and Jim kept bothering me, and I didn't have time to finish the project.
- ❍ It was impossible for me to save the money owed to you this week, but I'll have it by Tuesday.
- ❍ You have lots of money, so quit bugging me about the money I owe you.
- ❍ The publicity for the dance isn't finished. I'll get busy right away and complete it.
- ❍ No one reads posters and handbills, so that's why I didn't do them.

Values in My Life (4.12)

The following is a list of items. Some may be of value to you, and some may not. Read the list and choose the three most important to you. What is your reason for selecting them? Put the entire list in your order of priority.

1. To live in a larger home.
2. To rid the world of hunger.
3. To become famous.
4. To be a very rich person.
5. To be the President of the United States.
6. To be the prettiest or the most handsome person.
7. To have someone to do all of your homework for you.
8. To be elected president of a student organization.
9. To earn all As on your report card.
10. To have a life without illness or accident.
11. To have the best sports car.
12. To travel around the world.
13. To have a computer which will answer every question you ask it.
14. Other:

Susan and her Decision (5.2)

As President of the Student Council, Susan feels a real responsibility to reach out to all students. She feels that too few students in the school are actively involved in activities sponsored by the council. She must make some decisions about how to get more students aware of student activities, actively involved, and committed to making the Student Council events a success.

Susan knows that she needs some concrete facts to help her make decisions about student attitudes, the kind of activities students want, and how to motivate people to become more active in school affairs. How should she proceed?

A Critical Decision (5.6)

The Booster Club has a budget of $1500.00 each year. Of that, $700.00 comes from dues and $800.00 from fund raisers. Seven months have passed, and the club has spent $700.00, but it has raised only $100 through fund-raising activities. There are five months remaining in the year, and something must be done fast.

The president appeals to his officers. These are the suggestions that are offered. What would be the wisest course of action?

1. Stop spending and have no further activities for the rest of the year.
2. Increase the number of dues-paying members.
3. Increase the amount of the dues.
4. Have additional fund-raisers.
5. Ask the Student Council for a special allocation.

Brainstorming (6.3)

1. Express no negative evaluation of any ideas presented.
2. Work for quantity, not quality. The longer the list of ideas, the better.
3. Expand on each other's ideas; elaborate whenever possible.
4. Encourage zany, far-out ideas.
5. Record each idea, at least by a key word or phrase.
6. Set a time limit and hold strictly to it.

Summary of Parliamentary Procedure (6.4)

1. The purpose of parliamentary procedure is to maintain order.
2. The chairperson sets the pattern of conduct for the meeting.
3. The chairperson should summarize the discussions to date, but he/she should not dominate the conversation by offering his/her own opinions.
4. Only one speaker can be recognized at a time.
5. Only one main motion is allowed on the floor at any given time.
6. All motions must be seconded.
7. All remarks should be discussed by the group.
8. All motions must be voted on by the group.
9. A motion to adjourn can be made at any point in the meeting when the floor is not being held by a speaker.

The Student Council (6.8)

Susan has been elected President of the Student Council. The first item of business to come before her is the allocation of money for various student groups. Each group has a representative that appears before the council to plead their case.

The Drama Club feels that they should have the largest amount, because it has been five years since they have been able to put on a major production. The Literary Club feels that their needs are the greatest since they hope to publish an annual featuring student works. The Athletic Club needs new uniforms for the football team and feels that they should have the largest allocation. The French Club wants to sponsor a foreign exchange student and feels that their share of school funds should be increased accordingly.

Susan and her council must decide how the student activities budget will be divided, while trying to be fair to everyone.

A Task to Be Accomplished (6.15)

The Student Council is in charge of the school's annual spring dance. As President, Susan is the person who is responsible for everything running smoothly. All she can think of are all of the countless things that have to be done: hiring a band, decorations, door prizes, refreshments, etc. Put yourself in Susan's place and decide upon a course of action.

Steps for Solving Problems (7.1)

Step 1. Identify the problem.
Step 2. Generate all possible alternatives for action.
Step 3. Make a decision based upon the most promising alternatives.
Step 4. Develop and implement an action plan.
Step 5. Evaluate the results. (If the evaluation is not positive, go back to Step 2.)

Difficult Situations (8.17)

1. A member of the club is not completing their duties, and the president must talk with this individual.
2. The president must choose one person to head the finance committee. Two members want the position very much, and they are best friends.
3. The student paper published an editorial which greatly angered the school's administration. The club has gone on record supporting the staff of the paper and their right to freedom of speech. The officers of the club have been called to the principal's office of defend their stand.
4. Through a scheduling error, two student groups have been allowed to plan major activities on the same day. The vice-president must resolve the conflict.

Do I Have Planning Skills? (9.1)

	Yes	**No**
I can set goals.	____	____
I can set objectives for each goal.	____	____
I can plan activities in sequence.	____	____
I can eliminate time-wasting activities.	____	____
I have a tendency to procrastinate.	____	____
I can delegate authority to others.	____	____
I can identify persons who can help.	____	____
I can pace myself so I don't "burn out."	____	____

Plan for Leadership (9.17)

Goal:

Objectives	Activities	Time	Responsible	Person Evaluation

References

Abel, T., & Karnes, F. A. (1993). Self-perceived strengths in leadership abilities between suburban and rural gifted students using the Leadership Strengths Indicator. *Psychological Reports, 73*, 687-690.

Abramson, M. A. (1996). In search of the new leadership. *Management.* Retrieved from www.leadership.com

Aburdene, P., & Naisbitt, J. (1992). *Megatrends for women.* New York: Irvington Publishers.

Addison, L. (1985). *Leadership skills among the gifted and talented.* ERIC Clearinghouse, National Institution of Education (ERIC Document Reproduction Service No. ED 262 511).

Alvino, J. (1989). Psychological type: Implications for gifted. *Gifted Children Monthly, 10*(4), 1-2, 23.

Argulewicz, E. W., Elliott, S. W., & Hall, R. (1982). Comparison of behavioral ratings of Anglo-American and Mexican-American gifted children. *Psychology in the Schools, 19*, 469- 472.

Barr, L., & Barr, N. (1989). *The leadership equation.* Austin, TX: Eakin Press.

Bass, B. M. (1981). *Stogdill's handbook of leadership: A survey of theory and research.* New York: Free Press.

Bennett, W. J. (1986). *What works: Research about teaching and learning.* Washington, DC: U.S. Department of Education.

Bennis, W. G., & Nanus, B. (1985). *Leaders: The strategies for taking charge.* New York: Harper & Row.

Bisland, A. (2004). Developing leadership skills in young, gifted students. *Gifted Child Today, 27*(1), 24-29.

Bisland, A., Karnes, F. A., Cobb, Y. B. (2004). Leadership education. *Gifted Child Today, 27*(1), 50-57.

Black, J. D. (1984). *Leadership: A new model particularly applicable to gifted youth.* ERIC Clearinghouse, National Institution of Education (ERIC Document Reproduction Service No. ED 253 990).

Blake, R. R., & Mouton, J. S. (1985). *The managerial grid III.* Houston, TX: Gulf Publishing.

Boccia, J. A. (Ed.). (1997). *Students taking the lead: The challenges and rewards of empowering youth in schools.* San Francisco: Jossey-Bass.

Brooms, D., Clark, J., & Smith, M. (2018). *Empowering Men of Color on Campus: Building*

Student Community in Higher Education. New Brunswick; Camden; Newark; New Jersey; London: Rutgers University Press.

Burke, J. P., Harworth, C. E., & Ware, W. B. (1982). Scale for rating behavioral characteristics of superior students: An investigation of factor structure. *The Journal of Special Education, 16*(4), 477-485.

Calder, B. J. (1977). An attribution theory of leadership. In B. M. Staw & G. R. Salancik (Eds.), *New direction in organizational behavior.* Chicago: St. Clair Press.

Campbell, D., & Velsor, E. V. (1985). *The use of personality measures in the Leadership Development Program.* Greensboro, NC: Center for Creative Leadership.

Cattell, R. B., Cattell, M. D., & Johns, E. F. (1984). *Manual and norms for the High School Personality Questionnaire.* Champaign, IL: Institute for Personality and Ability Testing.

Chan, D. W. (2000). Developing the creative leadership training program for gifted and talented students in Hong Kong. *Roeper Review, 22*(2), 94-98.

Chauvin, J. C., & Karnes, F. A. (1983). A leadership profile of secondary gifted students. *Psychological Reports, 53,* 1259-1262.

Clark, K. E., & Clark, M. B. (1990). *Measures of leadership.* West Orange, NJ: Leadership Library of America.

Clark, K. E., & Clark, M. B. (1994). *Choosing to lead.* Charlotte, NC: Iron Gate Press.

Conradie, S. (1984). The identification of leadership potential. In J. Cawood, S. Conradie, C. Kapp, & J. Slabbert (Eds.), *Climbing the ladder to leadership: A panel discussion.* Paper presented at the international conference on education for the gifted, Ingenium 2000, Stellenbosch, South Africa. (ERIC Document Reproduction Service No. ED 292 228).

Delisle, D., & Delisle, J. (1996). *Growing good kids: 28 activities to enhance self-awareness, compassion, and leadership.* Minneapolis, MN: Free Spirit.

Delisle, J. R., & Espeland, P. (1999). *Kidstories: Biographies of 20 young people you'd like to know.* Minneapolis, MN: Econo-Clad Books.

Des Marias, J., Yang, Y., & Farzanehkia, F. (2000). Service-learning leadership development for youths. *Phi Delta Kappan, 81*(9), 678-681.

D'Ilio, V. R., & Karnes, F. A. (1992). Student leaders and their parents' perceptions of social skills. *Perceptual and Motor Skills, 74,* 863-866.

Eby, J. W. (1989). *Eby Gifted Behavior Index* (Administration manual). East Aurora, NY: D.O.K.

Elliott, S. N., & Argulewicz, E. W. (1983). Use of a behavior rating scale to aid in identification of developmentally and culturally different gifted children. *Journal of Psychoeducational Assessment, 1*(2), 179-186.

Ellis, J. L. (1990). *Leadership Strengths Indicator: A self-report leadership analysis instrument for adolescents.* Uniontown, NY: Royal Fireworks Press (formerly Trillium Press).

Ellis, J., Small-McGinley, J., & DeFabrizio, L. (2002). *Caring for kids in communities: Using mentorship, peer support, and student leadership programs in schools.* New York: Peter Lang Publishing.

Feldhusen, J. F., Hynes, K., & Richardson, W. B. (1977). Curriculum materials for vocational youth organizations. *Clearinghouse, 50*, 224-226.

Feldhusen, J. F., & Kennedy, D. M. (1986). Leadership training for gifted and talented youth. *Leadership Network Newsletter, 1*(2), 1-2.

Feldhusen, J. F., & Kennedy, D. M. (1988). Preparing gifted youth for leadership roles in a rapidly changing society. *Roeper Review, 10*(4), 226-230.

Fertman, C. I., & van Linden, J. A. (1999). Character education for developing youth leadership. *Education Digest, 65*(4), 11-17.

Fiedler, F. E. (1961). Leadership and leadership effectiveness traits. In L. Petrullo & B. M. Bass (Eds.), *Leadership and interpersonal behavior* (pp. 179-186). New York: Holt.

Florey, J. E., & Dorf, J. H. (1986). *Leadership skills for gifted middle school students.* ERIC Clearinghouse, National Institution of Education (ERIC Document Reproduction Service No. ED 273 404).

Foster, W. H., & Silverman, L. (1988). Leadership curriculum for the gifted. In J. VanTassel-Baska, J. Feldhusen, K. Seeley, G. Wheatley, L. Silverman, & W. Foster (Eds.), *Comprehensive curriculum for gifted learners* (pp. 356-360). Boston: Allyn & Bacon.

Fuller, R., Harrison, C., Bukstein, S., Martin, B., Lawerence, M., & Parks, C. (2017). The Impact of High School on the Leadership Development of African American Male Scholar-Athletes. *The High School Journal*, 100(2), 146-162.

Friedman, P. G., Friedman, R. J., & Van Dyke, M. (1984). Identifying the leadership gifted: Self, peer, or teacher nominations. *Roeper Review, 7*(2), 91-94.

Gallagher, J. J. (1982). *A leadership unit.* Uniontown, NY: Royal Fireworks Press (formerly Trillium Press).

Galton, F. (1869). *Hereditary genius: An inquiry into its laws and consequences.* London: Macmillan. (Paperback edition by Meridian Books, New York, 1962).

Gardner, H. W. (1983). *Frames of mind: The theory of multiple intelligences.* New York: Basic Books.

Gardner, J. W. (1990). *On leadership.* New York: Free Press.

Goertzel, V., Goertzel, M. G., Goertzel, T. G., & Hansen, A.M. W. (2003). *Cradles of eminence: Childhoods of more than 700 famous men and women.* Scottsdale, AZ: Great Potential Press.

Goleman, D. (1995). *Emotional intelligence: Why it can matter more than IQ.* New York: Bantam Books.

Haber-Curran, P., & Tillapaugh, D. (2017). Gender and student leadership: A critical examination. *New Directions for Student Leadership, 2017*(154), 11–22. https://doi.org/10.1002/yd.20236

Hagemann, B., & Newman, C. (1999). *Lead on!* Marion, IL: Pieces of Learning.

Hartman, R. K. (1969). *Teachers' identification of student leaders.* Unpublished paper, University of Connecticut.

Hensel, N. H. (1991). Social leadership skills in young children. *Roeper Review, 14*(1), 4-7.

Hersey, P., & Blanchard, K. H. (1982). Leadership style: Attitudes and behaviors. *Training and Development Journal, 36*(5), 50-52.

Hollander, E. P., & Offerman, L. (1990). Power and leadership in organizations: Relationships in transition. In K. E. Clark & M. B. Clark (Eds.), *Measures of leadership* (pp. 83-90). West Orange, NJ: Leadership Library of America.

Hollingworth, L. S. (1926). *Gifted children: Their nature and nurture.* New York: Macmillan.

House, C. (1980). *The leadership series.* Coeur d'Alene, ID: Listos.

Institute for Behavioral Research in Creativity. (1990). *Student talent and risk profile.* Salt Lake City, UT: Author.

Jacobs, T. O. (1970). *Leadership and exchange in formal organizations.* Alexandria, VA: Human Resources Research Organization.

Johns, E. F. (1984). The relationship of personality and achievement to creativity and leadership behavior. In R. B. Cattell, M. D. Cattell, & E. Johns (Eds.), *Manual and norms for the High School Personality Questionnaire.* Champaign, IL: Institute for Personality and Ability Testing.

Johnson, S. (2000). Recommendations for school leadership. *Gifted Child Today, 23*(2), 7-9.

Karnes, F. A. (1999). *The current effectiveness of the leadership studies program.* Unpublished manuscript, Hattiesburg, MS.

Karnes, F. A., & Bean, S. M. (1990). *Developing leadership in gifted youth* (Report No. EDO-EC-90-4). Reston, VA: Council for Exceptional Children. (ERIC Document Reproduction Service No. ED346082).

Karnes, F. A., & Bean, S. M. (1993). *Girls and young women leading the way.* Minneapolis, MN: Free Spirit.

Karnes, F. A., & Bean, S. M. (1995). *Leadership for students: A practical guide for ages 8-18.* Waco, TX: Prufrock Press.

Karnes, F. A., & Bean, S. M. (1996). Leadership and the gifted. *Focus on Exceptional Children, 29*(1), 1-12.

Karnes, F. A., Bean, S. M., & McGinnis, C. (1994/1995). Perceptions of leadership held by young females. *Journal of Secondary Gifted Education, 6*(2), 113-119.

Karnes, F. A., & Chauvin, J. C. (1985a). *Leadership Skills Inventory.* East Aurora, NY: D.O.K.

Karnes, F. A., & Chauvin, J. C. (1985b). *Leadership Skills Inventory activities manual.* East Aurora, NY: D.O.K.

Karnes, F. A., & Chauvin, J. C. (2000a). Leadership and the gifted in the 21st century. *Tempo, 20*(1), 1, 12-14.

Karnes, F. A., & Chauvin, J. C. (2000b). *Leadership Development Program.* Scottsdale, AZ: Great Potential Press (formerly Gifted Psychology Press).

Karnes, F. A., Chauvin, J. C., & Trant, T. J. (1984). Leadership profiles as determined by the HSPQ of students identified as intellectually gifted. *Roeper Review, 7*(1), 46-48.

Karnes, F. A., Chauvin, J. C., & Trant, T. J. (1985). Validity of the leadership potential score of the High School Personality Questionnaire with talented students. *Perceptual and Motor Skills, 61,* 163-166.

Karnes, F. A., Deason, D. M., & D'Illio, V. (1993). Leadership skills and self-actualization of school-age children. *Psychological Reports, 73,* 861-862.

Karnes, F. A., & D'Ilio, V (1988a). Assessment of concurrent validity of the Leadership Skills Inventory with gifted students and their teachers. *Perceptual and Motor Skills, 66,* 59-62.

Karnes, F. A., & D'Ilio, V. (1988b). Assessment of criterion-related validity of the Leadership Skills Inventory. *Psychological Reports, 62,* 263-267.

Karnes, F. A., & D'Ilio, V. (1989a). Leadership positions and sex-role stereotyping among gifted students. *Gifted Child Quarterly, 33*(2), 76-78.

Karnes, F. A., & D'Ilio, V. (1989b). Personality characteristics of student leaders. *Psychological Reports, 64,* 1125-1126.

Karnes, F. A., & D'Ilio, V. (1989c). Student leaders and social performance as measured by the Social Performance Survey Schedule. *Psychological Reports, 65,* 961-962.

Karnes, F. A., & D'Ilio, V. (1989d). Student leaders' and their parents' perceptions of the home environment. *Gifted Child Quarterly, 33*(4), 165-168.

Karnes, F. A., & D'Ilio, V. R. (1990a). Correlations between personality and leadership concepts and skills as measured by the High School Personality Questionnaire and the Leadership Skills Survey. *Psychological Reports, 66,* 851-856.

Karnes, F. A., & D'Ilio, V. R. (1990b). Sex-role stereotyping of leadership positions by student leaders. *Perceptual and Motor Skills, 70,* 335-338.

Karnes, F. A., & McGinnis, J. C. (1995). Looking for leadership. *Gifted Child Today, 18*(1), 30-35.

Karnes, F. A., & McGinnis, J. C. (1996). Scores on indicators of leadership skills, locust of control, and self-actualization for student leaders in grades 6 to 10. *Psychological Reports, 78,* 1235-1240.

Karnes, F. A., & Meriweather, S. (1988). Teacher trainers' views on leadership. *Gifted Child Today, 12*(1), 55-59.

Karnes, F. A., & Meriweather, S. (1989a). Developing and implementing a plan for leadership: An integral component for success as a leader. *Roeper Review, 11*(4), 214-217.

Karnes, F. A., & Meriweather, S. (1989b). Leadership development: Teachers' perceptions and practices. *Gifted Child Today, 12*(3), 50-53.

Karnes, F. A., & Meriweather-Bean, S. (1991). Leadership and gifted adolescents. In M. Bireley, & J. Genshaft (Eds.), *Understanding the gifted adolescent: Educational, developmental, and multicultural issues* (pp. 122-138). New York: Teachers College Press.

Karnes, F. A., Meriweather, S., & D'Ilio, V. (1987). The effectiveness of the Leadership Studies Program. *Roeper Review, 9*(4), 238-241.

Karnes, F. A., & Riley, T (1996). Perceptions of great leaders held by gifted youth. *Gifted Child Today, 19*(4), 14-15, 50.

Karnes, F. A., & Stephens, K. R. (1999a). Lead the way to leadership education. *Education Digest, 64*(8), 60-66.

Karnes, F. A., & Stephens, K. R. (1999b). Planning for the future: Leadership education in the schools. *Educational Horizons, 77*(2), 89-93.

Karnes, F. A., & Stephens, K. R. (2002). *Young women of achievement: A resource for girls in science, math, and technology.* Amherst, NY: Prometheus Books.

Karnes, F. A., & Zimmerman, M. (2001). Employing visual learning to enhance the leadership of the gifted. *Gifted Child Today, 24*(1), 56-59.

Khatena, J., & Morse, D. T. (1994). *Khatena-Morse Multi-talent Perception Inventory.* Bensonville, IL: Scholastic Testing Service.

Klimoski, R., & Amos, B. (2012). Practicing Evidence-Based Education in Leadership Development. *Academy of Management Learning & Education*, 11(4), 685-702.

Komives, S. R., Wagner, W., Slack, C., Owen, J. E., & Dugan, J. P. (2011). Formal Leadership Program Models. In *The Handbook for Student Leadership Development. 2nd edition* (pp. 231–234).

Landau, E., & Weissler, K. (1991). Tracing leadership in gifted children. *Journal of Psychology, 125*(6), 681-689.

Larson, R., & Angus, R. (2011). Adolescents' Development of Skills for Agency in Youth

Programs: Learning to Think Strategically. *Child Development*, 82(1), 277-294.

Lawrence, G. (1982). *People types and tiger stripes: A practical guide to learning styles.* Gainesville, FL: Center for the Applications of Psychological Type.

Lester, P., Hannah, S., Harms, P., Vogelgesang, G., & Avolio, B. (2011). Mentoring

Impact on Leader Efficacy Development: A Field Experiment. *Academy of Management Learning & Education*, 10(3), 409-429.

Leventhal, J. I. (1999). Providing leadership development for all students: An integral part of classroom instruction. *Tech Directions, 59*(1), 222-225.

Liang, C. T. H., Lee, S., & Ting, M. P. (2002). Developing Asian American leaders. *New Directions for Student Services, 97*, 81-89.

Lindsay, B. (1988). A lamp for Diogenes: Leadership giftedness and moral education. *Roeper Review, 1*(1), 8-11.

Lord, R. G., De Vader, C. L., & Alliger, G. M. (1986). A meta-analysis of the relation between personality traits and leadership perceptions: An application of validity generalization procedures. *Journal of Applied Psychology, 71*, 402-409.

MacGregor, M. G. (1999a). *Designing student leadership programs: Transforming the leadership potential of youth.* Denver, CO: Youthleadership.com.

MacGregor, M. G. (1997b). *Leadership 101: Developing leadership skills for resilient youth facilitator's guide.* Denver, CO: Youthleadership.com.

MacGregor, M. G. (1997c). *Leadership 101: Developing your leadership skills* (student workbook). Denver, CO: Youthleadership.com.

Magoon, R. A., & Jellen, H. G. (1980). *Leadership development: Democracy in action.* Poquoson, VA: Human Development Press.

Mariotti, J. (1999). The role of a leader. *Industry Week, 248*, 75.

McCarney, S. B. (1987). *Gifted Evaluation Scale.* Columbus, MO: Hawthorne Educational Services.

McCaulley, M. H., & the Staff of the Center for Applications of Psychological Type. (1990). The Myers-Briggs Type Indicator and leadership. In K. E. Clark & M. B. Clark (Eds.), *Measures of leadership* (pp. 381-419). New York: Center for Creative Leadership.

McNamara, J. F., Haensly, P. A., Lupkowski, A. E., & Edlind, E. P. (1985). *The role of extra-curricular activities in high school education.* Paper presented at the annual convention of the National Association for Gifted Children, Denver, CO. (Report prepared at the Gifted and Talented Institute, Texas A & M University, College Station, TX).

Meisgeier, C., & Murphy, E. (1987). *Murphy-Meisgeier Type Indicator for Children.* Palo Alto, CA: Consulting Psychologists Press.

Meriweather, S. (1989). *A study of leadership potential in middle school gifted students.* Unpublished doctoral dissertation, University of Southern Mississippi, Hattiesburg.

Meriweather, S., & Karnes, F. A. (1989). Toward the twenty-first century: Students' views on leadership. *Gifted Child Today, 12*(2), 40-43.

Merriman, J. E. (1999). Leadership conference. *Gifted Child Today, 22*(5), 18-28.

Milligan, J. (2004). Leadership skills of gifted students in a rural setting: Promising programs for leadership. *Rural Special Education Quarterly, 23*(1), 16-22.

Mitchel, J. V. (Ed.) (1985). *The Ninth Mental Measurements Yearbook.* Buros Institute of Mental Measurements. Lincoln, NE: The University of Nebraska Press.

Mumford, E. (1909). *The origins of leadership.* Chicago: University of Chicago Press.

Murphy, A. J. (1941). A study of the leadership process. *American Sociological Review, 6*, 674-687.

Myers, I. B., & McCaulley, M. (1985). *Manual: A guide to the development and use of the Myers-Briggs Type Indicator.* Palo Alto, CA: Consulting Psychologists Press.

Myers, I. B., & Myers, P. B. (1980). *Gifts differing.* Palo Alto, CA: Consulting Psychologists Press.

Myers, M. R., & Slavin, M. J. (1990). Emergence and maintenance of leadership among gifted students in group problem solving. *Roeper Review, 12*(4), 256-260.

Napier, L. A. (1995). Educational profiles of nine gifted American Indian women and their own stories about wanting to lead. *Roeper Review, 18*(1), 38-45.

Olivero, J. L. (1977). Leading leaders. In A. H. Passow (Ed.), *A new generation of leadership* (pp. 9-17). Ventura, CA: Ventura County Superintendent of Schools.

Owen, J. E. (2015). Connecting to Communities: Powerful Pedagogies for Leading for Social Change. In *Innovative Learning for Leadership Development* (pp. 85–94). essay, Jossey-Bass.

Parker, J. P. (1983). The Leadership Training Model: Integrated curriculum for the gifted. *Gifted Child Today, 29*, 8-13.

Parker, J. P. (1989). *Instructional strategies for teaching the gifted.* Boston: Allyn & Bacon.

Parker, J. P., & Begnaud, L. G. (2003). *Developing creative leadership.* Portsmouth, NH: Teacher Ideas Press.

Person, H. S. (1928). Leadership as a response to environment. *Education Records Supplement No. 6*, 9, 10-21.

Pleasants, R., Stephens, K. R., Selph, H., & Pfeiffer, S. (2004). Incorporating service learning into leadership education: Duke TIP's Leadership Institute. *Gifted Child Today, 27*(1), 16-22.

Plowman, P. D. (1981). Training extraordinary leaders. *Roeper Review, 3*, 13-16.

Posner, B. Z., Crawford, B., & Denniston-Stewart, R. (2015). A Longitudinal Study of Canadian Student Leadership Practices. *Journal of Leadership Education, 14*(2). https://doi.org/10.12806/v14/i2/r11

Ramey, D. A. (1991). Gifted leadership. *Roeper Review, 14*(1), 16-19.

Renzulli, J. S., Smith, F. H., White, A. J., Callahan, C. M., & Hartman, R. K. (1976). *Scales for Rating the Behavioral Characteristics of Superior Students* (SRBCSS). Wethersfield, CT: Creative Learning Press.

Richardson, W. B., & Feldhusen, J. F. (1987). *Leadership education: Developing skills for youth.* Uniontown, NY: Royal Fireworks Press (formerly Trillium Press).

Riley, T. L., & Brown, M. E. (1998). The magic of multimedia: Creating leaders of yesterday, today, and tomorrow. *Gifted Child Today, 21*(5), 20-26.

Riley, T. L., & Karnes, F. A. (1994a). A leadership profile of disadvantaged youth based on Leadership Strengths Indicator. *Psychological Reports, 74*, 815-818.

Riley, T. R., & Karnes, F. A. (1994b). Intellectually gifted elementary students' perceptions of leadership. *Perceptual and Motor Skills, 79*, 47-50.

Roach, A. D., Wyman, L. T., Brookes, H., Chavez, C., Heath, S. B., & Valdes, G. (1999). *Leadership giftedness: Models revisited.* Retrieved from www.nagc.org

Robbins, S. P. (1997). *Essentials of organizational behavior.* New York: Prentice Hall.

Roberts, J. L. (2004). Leadership is a "Must" for children who are gifted and talented. *Gifted Child Today, 27*(1), 5-6.

Roets, L. S. (1986a). *Leadership—A skills training program.* New Sharon, IA: Leadership Publications.

Roets, L. (1986b). *Roets Rating Scale for Leadership.* Des Moines, IA: Leadership Publishers.

Rudnitski, R. A. (1994). A generation of leaders for gifted education. *Roeper Review, 16*(4), 265-271.

Rush, M. C., Thomas, J. C., & Lord, R. G. (1977). Implicit leadership theory: A potential threat to the internal validity of leader behavior questionnaires. *Organizational Behavior and Human Performance, 20*, 93-110.

Schakel, L. (1984). *Investigation of the leadership abilities of intellectually gifted students.* Unpublished dissertation, University of South Florida, Tampa.

Schatz, E. M. (1981). *Development of an instrument to measure self-actualizing growth in adolescents.* Unpublished doctoral dissertation, University of Wisconsin.

Schriesheim, C. A., Tolliver, J. M., & Behling, O. C. (1984). Leadership theory: Some implications for managers. In W. E. Rosenbach & R. L. Taylor (Eds.), *Contemporary issues in leadership.* Boulder, CO: Westview Press.

Shankman, M. L., & Allen, S. J. (2010). *Emotionally intelligent leadership for students: Facilitation and activity.* John Wiley & Sons.

Shaunessy, E., & Karnes, F. A. (2004). Instruments for measuring leadership in children and youth. *Gifted Child Today, 27*(1), 42-47.

Sisk, D. A. (1984). Leadership as it relates to gifted education. *Gifted International, 2*(2), 130-148.

Sisk, D. A., & Rosselli, H. C. (1987). *Leadership: A special kind of giftedness.* Uniontown, NY: Royal Fireworks Press (formerly Trillium Press).

Sisk, D. A., & Shallcross, D. J. (1986). *Leadership: Making things happen.* Buffalo, NY: Bearly Limited.

Smith, D. L., & Smith, L. (1991). Exploring the development of leadership giftedness. *Roeper Review, 14*(1), 7-12.

Smyth, E., & Ross, J. A. (1999). Developing leadership skills of pre-adolescent gifted learners in small group settings. *Gifted Child Quarterly, 43*(4), 204-211.

St. John, E., Rowley, L., & Hu, S. (2009). Diversity and Leadership: A Study of High-Achieving Students of Color. *The Journal of Negro Education*, 78(1), 17-28.

Stogdill, R. M. (1974). *Handbook of leadership.* New York: Free Press.

Tannenbaum, A. J. (1983). *Gifted children: Psychological and educational perspectives.* New York: Macmillan.

Vroom, V., & Yetton, P. W. (1974). *Leadership and decision-making.* New York: Wiley.

Wade, R. C., & Putnam, K. (1995). Tomorrow's leaders? Gifted students' opinions of leadership and service activities. *Roeper Review, 18*(2), 150-151.

Waldman, D., Balthazard, P., & Peterson, S. (2011). Leadership and Neuroscience: Can We

Revolutionize the Way That Inspirational Leaders Are Identified and Developed? *Academy of Management Perspectives*, 25(1), 60-74.

Whorton, J. E., & Karnes, F. A. (1992). Comparison of parents' leadership styles: Perceptions of parents and student leaders. *Perceptual and Motor Skills, 74*, 1227-1230.

Wood, D., Larson, R., & Brown, J. (2009). How Adolescents Come to See Themselves as More

Responsible through Participation in Youth Programs. *Child Development*, 80(1), 295-309.

Yammarino, F. J., & Bass, B. M. (1990). Long-term forecasting of transformational leadership and its effect among naval officers: Some preliminary findings. In K. E. Clark & M. B. Clark (Eds.), *Measures of leadership* (pp. 151-169). West Orange, NJ: Leadership Library of America.

About the Author

Dr. Jane C. Chauvin is a Professor Emeritus of Education and Counseling at Loyola University New Orleans. Dr. Chauvin began her study of leadership during her doctoral studies, and her dissertation focused on the topic of leadership and gifted students. She has authored or co-authored several research articles focusing on leadership, and she continues to present locally and nationally on this topic. Dr. Chauvin's second research area is counseling, and she has published and presented in this area as well. She has served as the president of two national organizations and has been a member of several editorial boards in the fields of education and counseling.

CPSIA information can be obtained
at www.ICGtesting.com
Printed in the USA
JSHW041157020622
26475JS00003B/19